QUICK
kids'
QUILTS

QUICK *kids'* QUILTS

Easy-to-do
projects for newborns
to older children

Juju Vail

FIREFLY BOOKS

DEDICATION

To Ollie, Massimo, Tom, and Will for their inspiration.
And to Baby Q, who isn't here yet,
but won't let me forget that s/he's coming soon!

A FIREFLY BOOK

Published in Canada in 1999 by
Firefly Books Ltd.
3680 Victoria Park Avenue
Willowdale, Onrario M2H 3K

Published in the United States in 1999 by
Firefly Books (U.S.) Inc.
P.O. Box 1338, Ellicott Station
Buffalo, New York 14205

Cataloguing in Publication Data

Vail, Juju
Quick kids' quilts

Includes index.
ISBN 1-55209-350-6

1. Quilting. 2. Quilting—Patterns. 3. Children's quilt. I. Title.

TT835.V34 1998   746.46   C98-931808-7

This book was designed and produced by
Quintet Publishing Limited
6 Blundell Street
London N7 9BH

Creative Director: **Richard Dewing**
Art Director: **Clare Reynolds**
Designer: **Jacqui Ellis-Dodds**
Project Editor: **Toria Leitch**
Editor: **Maggie McCormick**
Photographer: **Joss Reiver Bany**
Illustrator: **Kate Simunek**

The Publishers acknowledge the financial support of the Government
of Canada through the Book Publishing Industry Development Program
for our publishing activities.

Typeset in Great Britain by
Central Southern Typesetters, Eastbourne
Manufactured in Singapore by Pica Separation Pte Ltd
Printed in Singapore by Star Standard Industries Pte Ltd

CONTENTS

Introduction

The arts of quiltmaking, patchwork, and appliqué have been with us for many generations. They have provided an opportunity for skilled needlewomen to display their talents while creating useful items for their homes and families. Today the value of needlework remains high; hand-made items, from our own childhood as well as our ancestors', are prized as family heirlooms. Consider what your child likes when making a quilt or other project especially for them, but consider also the durability and sentiment of the project, as it is destined to be an heirloom of the future.

The crafts in this book have been designed with this in mind. There are a variety of themes that can be adapted to match the tastes of any child (or parent), while special tips and techniques describe ideas to personalize your work.

Quick Quilting

Finding time to make a child's present by hand is difficult; parents and other family members juggle childcare with careers and a myriad of other activities. However, the quilts and other projects in this book are designed to be quick. They should all be achievable in the space of a weekend (provided you have one to spare), and many can be completed in just a few hours. Take an evening to prepare the project: cut the pieces and lay out the design, then complete it bit by bit in spare moments. You may prefer to make your project in a block of reserved time, benefiting from the quick machine quilting and appliqué techniques, or you may want to use basic hand stitches to make the work more leisurely and portable. Most projects can be adapted to either method.

To make sure you are efficient with your time, read through the instructions and equip yourself with all the necessary tools and materials before you begin. If templates or photographs need to be photocopied or enlarged, do this ahead of time.

▲ *Quilts need not be just for beds, this example called "Portrait of a Pilot" (see page 73) has been done on a 9 x 9-inch piece of fabric and is displayed in a picture frame.*

◄ *A detail from the House, Hearts, and Stars Quilt on page 94.*

Getting Started

The projects in this book are easy to make and many require only limited sewing experience. For each project, one of three skill levels is indicated. One star indicates a project that could be done by someone only experienced in hand mending, while two stars indicate a project suited to someone with some confidence in sewing techniques (someone able to sew simple curtains, for instance) and three stars indicate a

project suitable for a more experienced person, used to sewing garments. Familiarize yourself with the techniques in the following section. Quick quilting, sewing, piecing, appliqué, and decorating techniques used in this book are shown, as well as different methods for achieving similar results. The variety of methods can help you to select a way of working as well as a style to suit you. For instance, appliqué pieces can be secured by a machine zigzag stitch—this is

quick and very durable, but you may prefer to use a simple hand stitch which is more portable, and has a different aesthetic.

The projects are divided into three sections catering to different age ranges: cradle quilts, crib quilts, and bed quilts.

The first section offers nine projects that are suitable for newborn babies. It includes three small quilts, a mobile, wall pockets, a diaper hamper, a sleeping bag, and cushions for propping up a small baby.

The second section includes eight projects that are suitable for toddlers. The quilts are designed to fit in a crib, while instructions for an appliquéed sweatshirt, picture, hat, and soft toys are also included.

The final section offers designs for four single-bed quilts and four accompanying projects suitable for older children. These include a beanbag seat, a cloth book to make with a child, a drawstring bag, and a pillowcase.

Adapting Designs

All of the quilts in this book can be scaled up or down to fit larger or smaller bed sizes. This is achieved by enlarging or decreasing the size or quantity of the quilt's motif. Each project will offer a suggestion as to how this is most easily achieved. By altering the color scheme or introducing motifs from other designs in the book, you can customize your quilting project to your child's tastes and bedroom decorations. For instance,

the animal shapes used on the Animal Quilt (see page 76) could be substituted for the motifs used on the House, Hearts, and Stars Quilt (see page 94). Or, if you like, make your own motifs by making templates that will fit in with the size of the quilt squares.

Safety and Comfort

There are many safety controls and standards on purchased goods designed for children, and it is worth considering these when you make something yourself.

Most textile items designed for babies' bedrooms, such as curtains and blankets, have been treated with a fire retardant. You can buy fire-retardant sprays, but they can irritate sensitive skin and lungs. Natural fibers, such as cotton and wool, burn more slowly than synthetic fibers such as polyester, acrylic, and nylon, some of which leap toward a flame. It is not uncommon for children's fabrics to include a percentage of synthetic fiber for their easy-care qualities, but it is best to buy blends rather than 100% synthetic fabrics. For this reason you may also prefer to use cotton batting in your quilts. It is more expensive than polyester batting but it is worth investing in for the beautiful results it gives.

Small removable parts should also be avoided when making projects for the very young, particularly if the child is likely to be left alone and within reach of such items. Use zippers for closures instead of buttons or snaps, and decorate your projects with embroidery stitches instead of small decorations. Older children's projects may include small parts, but be sure they are well secured on the completed project.

Finally, many babies and young children have sensitive skin. Be wary of using dyes on fabrics that will touch their skin, and remember how uncomfortable scratchy wools were on your own skin when you were a child. If a fabric feels prickly to you, it is likely to feel even more so to a child.

Equipment and Techniques

Most of the projects in this book require very few tools. For some, such as the Humpty-Dumpty Sweatshirt on page 66, even a sewing machine is not necessary. However, a **sewing machine** will obviously speed up the making process of most needlecrafts. It does not need to be a fancy model, but should have a zigzag stitch as well as a straight stitch. A variety of accessories can be purchased to make work easier and faster. One accessory that is particularly helpful to the machine quilter is the **walking foot**. It reduces the uneven feeding of the layers in a quilt through the machine, which can cause wrinkling in the backing. A **transparent plastic foot** makes it easier to see when sewing a machine zigzag around appliquéed motifs.

Another piece of basic equipment is an **iron**. If yours does not have a steaming function, keep a spray bottle of water nearby for pressing cottons flat.

For cutting fabrics, all that is required is a good pair of **dressmaker's shears** ①, which should be kept sharp. However, a pair of small **embroidery scissors** ② next to your sewing machine is useful for snipping threads and trimming seams, while **pinking shears** ③ with serrated blades prevent fraying and can also create a decorative edge. If you plan to do a lot of patchwork, an expensive but excellent investment is a **rotary cutter** ④ and **self-healing mat**. They make cutting many pieces faster and more accurate. Be sure the blade is always covered when not in use and be particularly careful when using it around children. A **seam ripper** for opening seams that have been incorrectly stitched is also a useful addition to your tools.

③

①

④

②

A **tape measure** ⑤ and a **straight-edged metal ruler** are essential for measuring and cutting materials, while a **yardstick** will make cutting strips easier.

⑤ For tracing template pieces onto fabric, use a **soft pencil**. Mistakes can be erased with a **fabric eraser**. Designs can also be transfered using **dressmaker's carbon paper**, which comes in several colors, making it possible to transfer designs to both light and dark fabrics.

You also need a selection of needles to make different sewing tasks more efficient. Needles known as **sharps** are used for hand-sewing appliqué and patchwork, while **betweens** are useful for quilting and for making smaller stitches. **Crewel needles** have a larger eye and are therefore useful for working with embroidery threads. These come in sizes 1 to 10; 7 is recommended for the cotton-weight fabrics used in this book.

Machine sewing needles are numbered 70/10, 80/12, 90/14, etc. The finer the needle, the lower the number: 70/10 or 80/12 are suitable for both piecing and quilting with lightweight thread.

Special **quilter's pins** are longer than dressmaker's pins and can easily pass through several layers of fabric. **Safety pins** speed up the basting process when they are used instead of stitches to hold the layers of a quilt together before quilting.

The **thimble** is usually considered an essential piece of equipment to the quilter. However, since most of our quick quilts are held together with either machine quilting or tying, you may not find the need for one.

An **embroidery hoop** is useful for holding sections of appliqué taut while working it.

Any supplementary tools or equipment that are required for a project, but not mentioned here, will be listed with the project instructions.

Materials

Fabrics for children's quilts must be washable and colorfast. If you are unsure as to whether a fabric is **colorfast,** you can test it by leaving it to soak in a bucket of warm water with a small swatch of previously washed white cotton fabric. Leave to soak for 30 minutes, rinse with cool water, let it dry, and then compare your white swatch to the original white fabric to see if it picked up any of the colored fabric dye.

For the easiest, fastest, and most durable results, choose materials of similar weights that are not too thick. Most of the projects in this book were made with cotton material which is similar in weight to shirt or sheet fabric. Materials of this sort can usually be obtained in a wide variety of solid and patterned colors from fabric stores or mail-order quilting suppliers. Watch for mixed packs of cotton squares, which are ideal for making pieced quilts such as the folk art House, Hearts, and Stars quilt on page 94 or for using in small appliqués.

However, it is not always necessary to buy new fabrics. You can collect together scraps, remnants, or bits of old clothing. It may be appropriate to use a fabric from a loved garment that your child has outgrown.

Always wash fabrics before you begin— wash previously used cloth in hot water, and other fabrics at their regular washing temperature.

You will need a selection of colors in 100% cotton or polyester/cotton **sewing thread** for appliqué, piecing, and quilting.

It is also useful to have a variety of **embroidery threads** on hand. For hand embroidery choose pearl cotton, a high-sheen 2-ply thread, or stranded embroidery thread, which can be separated for fine work. **Machine embroidery threads** include silky rayons, and metallic and glitter threads.

Readymade **bias binding** saves a lot of time in finishing the edges of quilts and comes in a wide variety of colors and several widths. It is also a good idea to keep a selection of ribbons and **trims** on hand to decorate your projects.

Double-sided fusible bonding web seals two layers of fabric together and is often used to bond an appliqué motif to a ground fabric. A medium-weight **fusible interfacing** is useful for backing appliqué pieces that have a turned-under edge.

Batting, used for stuffing quilts and toys, is available in a variety of weights and fibers. Cotton batting has a beautiful drape, but it is more expensive than polyester batting which is durable and washes well.

There are also a number of other products for embellishing textiles that extend the decorative possibilities of the quick quilter. Fabric **dyes** can be used to overdye fabrics or painted directly onto materials to create patterns. **Fabric paints** come in a variety of colors and include such specialties as puffy, gloss, and sparkle paints, while **image transfer fluid** allows you to transfer photocopies onto your fabrics.

Sewing Basics

With right sides together (unless otherwise instructed), match the cut edges of fabric pieces, and take care to sew a straight and accurate seam using the seam allowance stated in the project instructions. Seams are stitched from one edge across to the other. Match corners, edges, and notches precisely.

Pairs of pieces can be **chained** one after another, but always make a stitch or two of thread between each pair so that they do not come undone when snipped apart later.

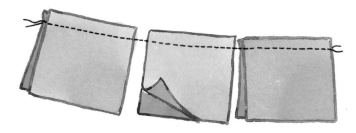

When sewing **curved seams**, the surplus fabric must be clipped so the shape will lie flat when the seam is turned right side out. Cut into concave curved edges at right angles, up to ⅛ inch from the seam. For convex curves, remove the excess fabric by cutting out evenly spaced small notches. The tighter the curve, the closer the cuts should be.

Always **press** seams before sewing the next unit across them. Patchwork seams are generally pressed to one side (toward the darker fabric), whereas construction seams such as those found in garments are pressed open. After trimming loose ends and threads from the back of a completed quilt top, give it a final press before assembling the quilt layers.

How to insert a zipper

1 Stitch the seam up to the zipper opening and press. Turn under the seam allowance for the zipper, baste, and carefully press the edges of the opening. Hold the zipper in position at the slider end and baste it down to the edges of the opening. Baste to both ends of the tape to anchor the zipper and keep it straight.

2 Set your machine to a straight stitch slightly larger than for the rest of the sewing. Attach the zipper foot and adjust to the correct position. Place the work under the foot, right-side up, ⅜ inch below the end of the zipper. Lower the needle and then the foot, and machine stitch very slowly to the end of tape. Repeat for the other side of the tape, readjusting the zipper foot position.

3 Stitch across the bottom, ⅜ inch below the zipper end. Remove all basting stitches.

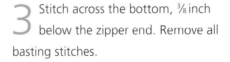

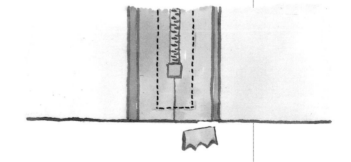

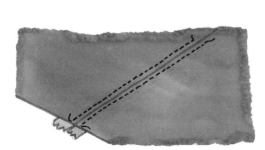

Appliqué

Appliqué features in this book because it is an effective and versatile way to decorate sewing projects. Traditional appliqué has a turned-under edge on each appliqué piece. This is straightforward to do but time-consuming. Double-sided fusible bonding web speeds up the process, but makes the area of the appliqué thicker. Appliqué pieces are fused directly to a ground fabric with bonding web. The edges do not need to be turned under since the web prevents the appliqué fabric from fraying.

Polar fleece and **felt fabrics** extend the quick appliqué techniques since neither fabric frays. Templates can simply be traced onto the polar fleece or felt, and the pattern piece cut out and then positioned on the background fabric and stitched in place using machine or hand stitching.

Appliqué with double-sided fusible bonding web

1 Trace the outline of the reversed appliqué template onto the fusible web backing paper.

2 Roughly cut the design from the fusible web and iron it to the wrong side of your appliqué fabric. Let it cool and then cut around the outline with a sharp pair of scissors.

3 Peel off the backing paper and iron your appliqué, with the fusible webbing side down, to the right side of your background fabric. If the appliqué design consists of several pieces, peel off all the backing papers, lay each piece in position, and then iron. Finish the appliqué by selecting an appropriate stitch to secure the appliqué piece.

Turned-edge appliqué

1 Trace the outline of the reversed appliqué template onto medium-weight interfacing and carefully cut out.

2 Iron the interfacing to the wrong side of your appliqué fabric. Draw a cutting line ¼ inch outside the interfacing outline and cut out your appliqué piece.

3 Turn under the edges and baste, clipping curves as necessary.

4 Position appliqué pieces on the ground fabric and pin in place. Finish the appliqué by selecting an appropriate stitch, such as slipstitch, to secure the appliqué piece.

Stitches

Turned-edge appliqué motifs must always be stitched to the background fabric. Any of the stitches described on pages 21–23 are suitable, as long as they are worked close enough to the edge of the motif to hold the seam allowance under after the basting stitch is removed. Traditionally a hand stitch would be

used, but a machine or embroidery stitch is also suitable and when you have a large motif, or a number of small ones, using a machine stitch obviously makes the job a lot quicker and easier.

If you are fusing appliqué motifs to a background fabric with fusible bonding, your stitch choice will depend on your appliqué fabrics. A fabric that does not fray such as felt or polar fleece requires no stitching and can be left as it is or decorated with embroidery stitches. Sturdy medium-weight cottons will probably not fray very much either and allow you to choose from whatever

stitch you prefer, while a loosely woven fabric is best secured with a machine zigzag stitch to prevent the edges from fraying—you can increase or decrease the density of the stitches according to how loosely woven your fabric is. To find out how stable your material is, fuse a 2-inch circle of the fabric to a swatch of ground fabric and put it through a wash cycle. If the edges have frayed a little, choose a stitch that will prevent fraying such as machine zigzag or hand satin stitch.

Machine Stitches

When stitching motifs by machine, work slowly and carefully, manipulating the fabric as it passes through the machine so that the foot is always parallel to the edge of the motif. Some machines are supplied with a transparent plastic foot which makes it easier to follow the needle.

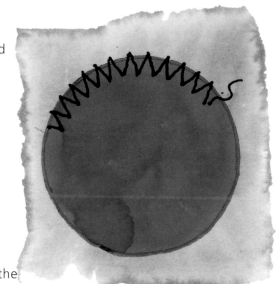

The **zigzag** controls on the sewing machine can be set in several ways to produce a stitch that covers the cut edge of an appliqué motif (above). A narrow open zigzag allows some of the fabric to show through, while a wide, closely set **satin stitch** (left) is dense enough to hide the edge completely. Using a thread that matches your appliqué fabric will hide your stitching, while a contrasting thread can accentuate the design lines of your appliqué. Experiment on scraps of fabric to get the effect you want.

An ordinary machine **straight stitch** (right) can be used for sewing fabrics that do not fray, such as felt or dense cotton applied with fusible bonding. Set stitch length slightly shorter than for seaming to give a more flexible line. Stitch just inside the motif and keep the needle a steady ⅛ inch from the edge, using the presser foot as a guide.

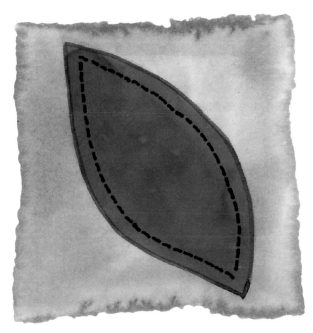

Hand Stitches

Running stitch is used when the line of stitching is intended to show, and it can be worked in a contrasting color if required. The length of the individual stitches can vary according to the scale of the work. This is probably the easiest stitch to do, but needs to be done carefully to ensure the stitches are of an even length.

Slipstitch gives an almost invisible seam and is the neatest finish if you wish to hide the stitching. Make small, neat stitches, no more than ¼ inch apart, being careful not to pull the thread too tight. Bring the needle up just inside the motif, then back over the appliqué edge and through the background fabric.

Overcasting is best used for fabrics that may fray, even when applied with fusible bonding, such as those with a loose weave which includes most cotton fabrics. The thread overlaps the edge of the motif and prevents the fabric from fraying.

Embroidery Stitches

Backstitch produces a solid outline. It can be used to hold a motif in place on a background fabric or as decoration. Backstitch is worked from right to left. Make a row of small stitches, taking the needle back to the end of the previous stitch each time.

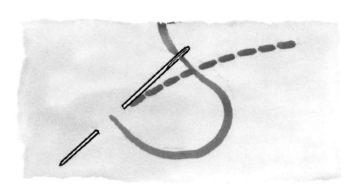

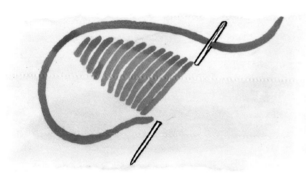

Satin stitch has a smooth finish and is used to fill shapes and outline motifs. Begin work at the center of the shape to be filled and work out to each end of it, or work all around the edge of an appliqué motif. Try to keep an even edge.

French knots can be worked in clusters or singly. Bring the thread through and, keeping it taut with your thumb, twist the needle around it twice. Insert the needle back through the fabric close to the starting point and pull it through to form a knot.

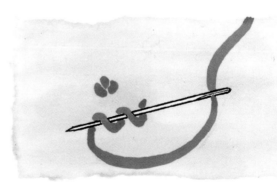

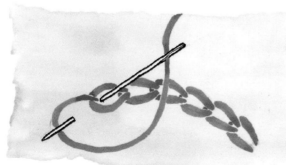

Chain stitch is used to fill shapes or as an outline stitch. You can also work single stitches to form small flower petals. Work the stitches from top to bottom or curving from right to left.

Textile Decoration

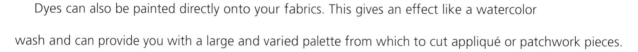

Traditionally fabric choice, stitching, and appliqué were relied upon to decorate a quilt top. While these are all very effective ways of embellishing, there are faster methods available through modern dyes, paints, and transfer products.

Fabric dyes can be used to overdye patterned fabrics, changing the colors slightly. If you like a homespun look, you can dye them in a strong solution of **tea**.

Dyes can also be painted directly onto your fabrics. This gives an effect like a watercolor wash and can provide you with a large and varied palette from which to cut appliqué or patchwork pieces.

Be sure to rinse and wash fabrics thoroughly after dyeing them. Check that the dyes are completely colorfast (see page 14).

Fabric paints come in a huge choice of colors and textures. Puff paints and glitter sticks are available along with traditional fabric paints. Nontoxic paints are suitable for letting children make their own images on fabric, which can then be pieced together in a quilt. Even young children can make hand- and footprints.

If you are confident about painting directly onto fabrics, you can make your own motifs or use stencils and printing objects such as leaves to transfer a design to fabric.

Image transfer

Transfering photographs and illustrations to fabric is a quick and easy way to make a unique design. Photocopied images can easily be transfered to fabric with an image transfer fluid such as Dylon's Image Maker or by copying images onto heat transfer paper, available from photocopy suppliers. Since image transfer fluid is widely available through craft and art suppliers, it has been used in the projects in this book.

Making a photocopy for transfering

To transfer an image you must first make a good-quality color or black and white photocopy. If you are photocopying a black and white design, such as those included in the project on page 41, copy it on white or cream paper, whichever matches your fabric most closely.

To make a color copy from a **photograph**, choose a well-lit, matt print. You may also find good-quality images in magazines or books, but remember that it may be illegal to reproduce certain pictures without prior permission, due to copyright law.

Transfering photocopies to fabric reverses the image. Therefore, images including **words or numbers** should be reversed using the photocopier reverse function before being transfered to your chosen fabric.

To **enlarge** a photocopy to the correct size before transfering, calculate the percentage of increase required. The percentage has already been calculated for the designs in this book, but you may wish to change the scale or use an image of your own choosing. Measure the height of your original and call this X. Decide what height you would like the photocopied image to be; this dimension is Y. Multiply X by 100 and then divide by Y. This number is the percentage of increase. Most photocopiers will increase in increments of one up to 200%.

Cut your image from the photocopy carefully, removing as much of the excess paper as possible. Transfer your photocopy following the directions given by the manufacturer.

Transfering a color copy to a colored ground fabric

If you wish to transfer a color copy to a ground fabric that is not white or cream, you will need to prepare the area first. Place your image face down on the fabric, and trace around it with a pencil. Paint the area inside the pencil mark with white fabric paint, let it dry and then set according to the instructions given by the paint manufacturer. You can then transfer your picture with the image transfer fluid.

Patterns and Templates

Full-size patterns have been supplied wherever possible. However, due to size constraints, some patterns have been scaled down. The easiest way to make a full-size pattern is to enlarge it on a photocopier. Pattern pieces supplied for garments, bags, hats, and toys include notches, construction markings, seam allowances, and grain-line markings. **Notches** and double notches are used to indicate where pattern pieces match together. **Construction markings**, such as slash lines and zipper and pocket placements, are indicated on the pattern piece and can be transferred to the fabric with a sharp pencil piercing the pattern piece. **Seam allowances** indicate how far to sew from the fabric edge. It is important to cut all pattern pieces with their **grain-line** arrows parallel to the selvage edge of the cloth (see illustration above), otherwise the final piece may not lay nicely flat.

Pattern pieces for quilt blocks and appliqués must be made into **templates** for tracing on fabric. Appliqué templates do not include seam allowances. Appliqué motifs, which will be used just once, can be cut directly from the photocopy. But if the motif repeats, the outline should be transferred to thin cardboard or template plastic for a more durable template. Label it and identify the right side. Templates traced onto **double-sided bonding** will make appliqué motifs in reverse. Fuse them to the wrong side of your fabric.

Assembling Quilt Layers

The process of binding quilt layers to one another with decorative quilting stitches is slow and laborious. All the quilts in this book make use of faster techniques such as stitch-in-the-ditch, outline quilting, tying, or placed embroidery. None of these quilting patterns needs to be marked on the quilt before you assemble the layers.

Two methods are used for finishing the edges of the quilt: bagging out and binding the edges. When bagging out a quilt, the layers are basted together ready for quilting **after** the quilt has been turned right side out.

Bagging out

This is a quick method to finish the edges of a quilt. When bagging out, you do not need to add in a binding as well.

1 Lay the batting out. Lay the backing fabric on top of the batting, right side up, then lay the quilt top, right side down, on top.

2 Trim the backing fabric and the batting to the same size as the quilt top. Pin the layers together, then stitch around the edge of the quilt, leaving a gap long enough to turn the quilt right side out.

3 Trim the batting close to the seam line, then turn the quilt so the batting is in the middle of the sandwich. Close the opening with small invisible slipstitch.

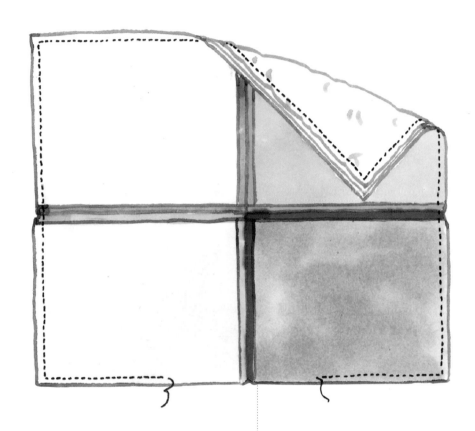

Layering a quilt

1 Press the backing fabric and spread it right side down on a flat surface. Center the batting on top, smoothing out any wrinkles without stretching it. Center the prepared quilt top, right side up, on the batting. If you need to re-position the quilt top, do not drag it over the batting. Lift it carefully to avoid wrinkling the batting and backing.

2 Pin the layers together starting from the center and working out.

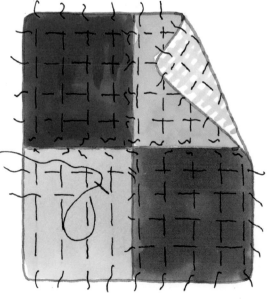

Basting

This can be done with thread or stainless steel safety pins. When using thread, use a long piece of thread and start in the middle. Baste out to the edge in rows of 4-inch intervals in both directions. Safety pins should be placed at closer intervals.

Binding a quilt

Binding should be done when the quilting is complete. Bias binding can be bought in several widths and a variety of colors, and is much faster to use than making a binding yourself. A hem should be pressed along one side of the binding before you begin to attach it to your quilt.

1 Place the binding right sides together on the quilt, matching raw edges, beginning along one side, not at a corner. Fold up the beginning of the binding and pin and stitch the binding in place until exactly ¼ inch from the corner.

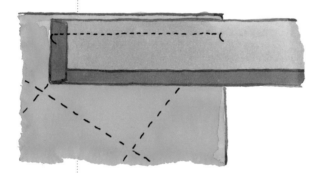

2 Backstitch a short distance, then remove the quilt from the machine. Fold the binding up at a 45-degree angle, then back down to align it with the adjacent edge of the quilt top, giving you the bulk to fold the binding to the back. Make sure the folds are sharp and exactly in line with the edges of the quilt top.

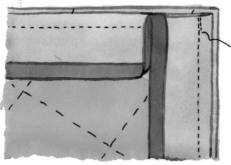

3 Pin and stitch, repeating the process to turn the remaining corners neatly. At the end, allow enough binding to overlap the beginning, and trim away any excess. Continue stitching through the overlap to secure the binding where it meets.

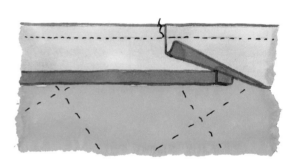

4 Fold the binding to the back of the quilt, and hem in place along the stitching line.

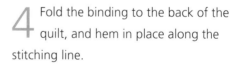
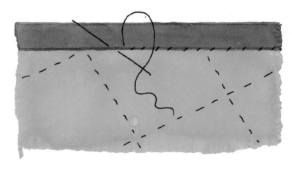
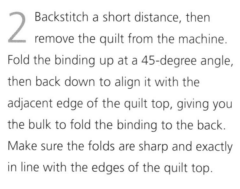

Quilting

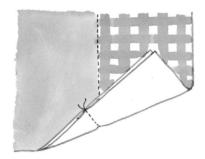

Several simple techniques are used to hold quick quilt layers together.

To **stitch-in-the-ditch**, a machine straight stitch quilts the layers along the seam lines of pieced blocks or immediately next to appliqué motifs. A transparent plastic foot for your machine makes it easier to follow the ditch.

Outline quilting is done approximately ¼ inch away from seam lines of motifs or quilt blocks. It can be marked with a pencil or masking tape or followed with the eye.

Tying a quilt is a quick way of permanently securing the layers. The knot can be on either the back or the top as a decorative feature. On the opposite side you will see a small stitch of the tying thread, so bear this in mind when choosing the color of thread. Use a thick thread such as pearl cotton and a sharp needle with a large eye.

1 Starting in the center of the place where you wish to position the tie, take a stitch through all three layers and pull the thread through, leaving a tail at least 6 inches long. Re-enter the quilt at the point where the next tie is to be and take another small stitch.

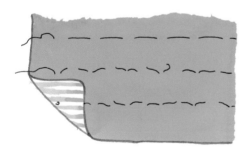

2 Repeat, without cutting until there is a stitch in each of the places to have a tie.

3 Cut the thread between stitches, then tie the thread using a square knot.

Signing your work

You should finish your work with an inscription label, including your name, date, and possibly a dedication to the child you have made it for. Labels can be embroidered by hand, cross stitched, machine embroidered, painted with fabric paints, or simply written with indelible fabric pens. Press under the seam allowance of the label and stitch it neatly to the back of the quilt or inside of the garment.

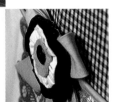

cradle quilts

These projects are for newborn babies. The quilts are an

ideal size for tucking into a buggy or swaddling a baby.

They all make excellent gifts for an expectant mother.

Tree of Life Quilt

DIFFICULTY
RATING: ✲ ✲

31 x 31 inches

This charming quilt is not difficult or time-consuming to make. To make it bigger, increase the size of the templates on a photocopier and/or increase the checked border.

Materials

- *White and colored cotton for border squares*
- *1 yard of fusible bonding web*
- *Scraps of bright-colored and/or printed fabrics for appliqué*
- *21-inch square piece of cotton for background of center panel*
- *Sewing threads to match appliqué fabrics*
- *1 yard of batting*
- *1 yard of white cotton backing fabric*
- *4 yards of double-fold binding*
- *Pearl cotton for tying quilt*

Instructions

Note: All seam allowances are ¼ inch unless otherwise stated.

MAKING THE BORDER

1 The border for this quilt is made of white and colored check squares. Using the template on page 120, cut 40 white and 40 colored or patterned squares of fabric.

2 Sew the squares together in 4 strips of 12 and 4 strips of 8 squares, alternating a colored square with a white one. Lay them on the floor first to check that you are happy with the balance of colors. Press the seams flat.

3 Sew the strips together, matching all seams to make two long checked borders for the sides of the quilt and two short borders for the top and bottom. Press all seams flat at the back of the work.

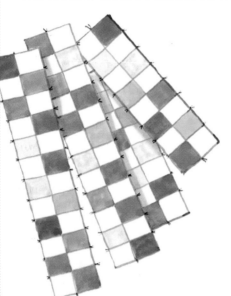

MAKING THE CENTER PANEL

4 Enlarge the templates on a photocopier by 200% and then trace them on the fusible bonding web. Iron the bonding to the wrong side of the appliqué fabrics and carefully cut the shapes out.

5 Position the appliqué pieces on the background, using the diagram as a guide. Press in place. Using matching thread, zigzag the appliqués in place.

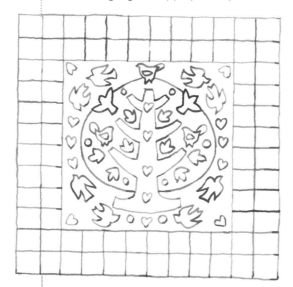

ASSEMBLING THE QUILT TOP

6 With edges and right sides together, sew the top and bottom borders to the center quilt panel. With edges and right sides together, sew the side borders to the quilt. Press all seams flat.

▼ *The tree of life is an inspirational motif for a newborn baby.*

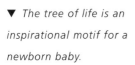

ASSEMBLING THE QUILT LAYERS

7 Assemble the quilt layers and baste them together.

8 Trim the bottom layers to within ¼ inch of the top piece. Bind edges with the double-fold binding (see page 28 for technique).

9 Tie the quilt at the seam corners, with the bows at the back of the quilt.

Hearts and Stars Wall Pockets

DIFFICULTY
RATING: ✱ ✱

11 x 24½ inches

Wall pockets are handy for storing diaper changing accessories above a changing table. When your child grows up, the pockets can be used to store toys that are no longer played with. The shape of the pockets means that they could even be used to keep shoes tidy and out of the way.

Materials

- ¼ yard of four different cotton fabrics
- Fusible bonding web
- Scraps of bright-colored and/or printed fabrics for appliqués and triangle pendants
- ½ yard of gingham for the pocket lining and pleats
- ¼ yard of medium-weight fusible interfacing
- ½ yard of two different cotton fabrics for the pocket background and backing
- ½ yard of batting
- 2 yards of double-fold bias binding
- Three buttons
- Sewing threads to match appliqué fabrics

Instructions

Note: All seam allowances are ⅝ inch unless otherwise stated.

MAKING THE WALL POCKETS

1 Cut four pocket fronts of 6½ x 8½ inches each from different fabric. Trace two heart and two star templates, found on page 120, onto the fusible bonding web and iron them to the wrong side of your appliqué fabrics. Fuse the appliqués to the right side of your pockets, centering them.

2 Cut three pieces of 6½ x 8½ inches and two pieces of 3½ x 8½ inches from the gingham fabric for the pocket pleats. With edges and right sides together, sew the pocket pleats to the sides of the pocket fronts, starting and finishing with the narrower pocket pleats. Press seams open.

3 For the pocket lining, cut a strip 8½ x 46 inches from the gingham fabric and interfacing. Fuse the interfacing to the wrong side of the lining fabric. With edges and right sides together, sew the pocket lining along the top edge to the pocket fronts and pleats. Fold the pocket lining to the inside of the pocket and press the seam. Baste the lining in place.

4 Pleat the pockets by folding the pocket fronts together in the center of each pocket pleat, hiding the gingham. Baste along the top and bottom of pleats.

MAKING THE BACKGROUND

5 Cut a rectangle of 10½ x 24½ inches from a piece of colored cotton for the wall pocket background. Cut two more pieces the same size from the batting and another piece of colored cotton for the backing. Baste the layers together with the backing, wrong side up, on the bottom, then the batting and finally the pocket background, right side up, on top.

6 With edges together and the lining next to the wall pocket background, pin and baste the pockets to the sides and bottom of the background. Remove the basting stitches holding the pocket pleats in place and sew the center of each pleat to the background fabric.

MAKING THE TRIANGLE PENDANTS

7 Make nine pendants from colored fabric scraps by cutting two triangular shapes for each, using the template on page 120. With edges and right sides together, sew each of the triangles together with a ¼-inch seam allowance, leaving the short side open. Clip the points off the seam allowance and turn the triangles right side out. Press seams flat.

8 With edges together and triangle points facing up, pin all the triangles at equal distances to the back of the pocket background. Machine baste in place.

9 Keeping the triangle points facing up and out of the way, sew the binding to the outside edge of the background, catching the wall pockets and their pleats in the seam. Press the triangle pendants down and topstitch the binding so the triangle points face down and are visible on the right side of the hanging.

MAKING THE STRAPS

10 Cut 3 strips of colored fabrics, each 4 x 8 inches. Cut three strips the same size from medium-weight interfacing. Fuse the interfacing to the wrong side of the straps.

11 With right sides together, fold the straps in half lengthwise and stitch around two edges. Turn the strap right side out and fold under the remaining seam allowance. Slipstitch in place. Press.

12 Sew one end of each strap to the backing just below the binding, at equal distances. Fold the strap over to the front and anchor it in place with a button in the middle.

▼ *Use the pockets to tidy away toys and teddy bears.*

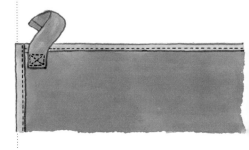

Birds and Hearts Mobile

DIFFICULTY
RATING: ★

31 x 31 inches

This bright mobile will amuse babies and adults. Adding bells and sequins will bring sound and light to your mobile, but they mean that it must be hung out of a baby's reach. If you want your mobile to be more interactive, do not use removable trims.

Materials

- *10 inches of muslin or scrap cotton fabric*
- *12 inches of fusible bonding web*
- *10 inches of batting*
- *Scraps of bright-colored and/or printed fabrics for appliqué*
- *Sewing threads to match appliqué fabrics*
- *7-inch diameter metal ring (available from craft shops)*
- *½ yard of ¼-inch wide green gingham ribbon*
- *½ yard of ¼-inch wide red ribbon*
- *Assortment of beads, sequins, bells, and tassels for decoration*
- *6 inches each of three different-colored narrow ribbons*
- *2 yards of ⅝-inch wide red gingham ribbon*
- *14 inches of 3-ply satin cord*
- *Colored elastic thread*

Tools & Equipment

- *White craft glue*

MAKING THE BIRDS AND HEARTS

1 Cut two pieces of muslin or scrap cotton fabric, two pieces of fusible bonding web, and one piece of batting 10 inches square. Layer them in a sandwich with the muslin pieces on each side, followed by the bonding and then the batting in the center. Iron together.

2 Make the bird and heart shapes by tracing around the inside line of the appliqué templates, enlarging to the size you want. Using these templates, trace three bird shapes and four heart shapes on the muslin and cut out.

3 Make a second set of bird and heart templates by tracing around the outer line of the pattern. Trace six bird shapes (reversing the template for half of them) and eight heart shapes onto fusible bonding web and iron to scraps of cotton fabric.

4 To make the stuffed appliqués, fuse one layer of the appliqué shape with a layer of the batted muslin shape and a second appliqué shape together with the bonding sides inside the sandwich. Iron together and machine zigzag around the outside of the shape. Repeat until you have three stuffed birds and four stuffed hearts.

5 Decorate each bird with beads for eyes, tassels on tails, and a bell and ribbon bow at the bottom. If you wish, decorate the hearts with sequins, tassels at the bottom of three, and a bell and ribbon at the bottom of the fourth.

MAKING THE PADDED RING

6 Cut a long length of 1-inch wide batting and wrap it around the ring, stitching from beginning to end to hold it in place.

7 Wrap the red gingham ribbon around the ring in the same way, overlapping slightly. Stitch from beginning to end to hold it in place.

ASSEMBLING THE MOBILE

8 Put a dot of white craft glue at the end of the 3-ply satin cord to prevent it from unraveling. When the glue is dry, make a loop with the first 4 inches of the cord, securing it in place with a couple of stitches and another drop of glue.

9 Separate the rest of the cord's three plys into individual strands. Attach the end of each strand to the metal ring at equal spaces by looping around the ring, holding it with a few stitches and then securing with a drop of glue.

10 String the birds and hearts with 4-inch lengths of elastic. Knot and sew these to the ring. Hide each seam with a ribbon.

▼ *Use a contrasting colored thread to stitch around the appliqué shapes, for added decoration.*

Antique Buggy Quilt

DIFFICULTY
RATING: *

30 x 38 inches

This is an ideal quilt size for tucking into a buggy. If you prefer another color scheme to the black and white used here, take copies of the illustrations provided, using a color copier, in your preferred palette. The reverse side is made from waterproof fabric so the quilt can also be used as a portable changing mat.

If you want the quilt to fit a standard crib, increase the size of the central panel to 20 x 27½ inches and enlarge the border pieces until they give a finished dimension of 35 x 45 inches. Don't use waterproof fabric on this quilt.

Materials

- *½ yard of ivory cotton fabric*
- *Image transfer fluid*
- *¼ yard of black and white gingham*
- *¼ yard of black and white floral fabric*
- *Ivory sewing thread*
- *1 yard of batting*
- *1 yard of waterproof fabric*
- *¼ yard of black cotton fabric*
- *Black sewing thread*
- *Pink embroidery floss*

Instructions

Note: All seam allowances are ⅝ inch unless otherwise stated.

▲ *Enlarge x 250%*

TRANSFERING THE IMAGES TO THE CREAM COTTON

1 Make four photocopies of the bow design (below left) and carefully cut each one out so there is very little white paper around the edges. Enlarge the buggy so it fills an 11 x 16-inch sheet of paper and cut it out.

2 Cut four pieces of the ivory cotton into 10 x 12-inch rectangles. Transfer the bow designs to these cotton pieces following the directions given with the image transfer fluid. Be sure to keep the grain line parallel with the middle of the bow pattern; draw a light pencil line on the wrong side of the photocopy to indicate the middle line of the bow and align this with the grain. When the images are transfered, cut the

rectangles down to 8⅜ x 10¼ inches, keeping the image centered in the block.

3 Transfer the buggy image (below) to an ivory cotton rectangle of 16 x 24 inches, keeping the grain line parallel to the center of the transfer.

When the image is transfered, trim the rectangle to 14¼ x 19¾ inches, keeping the image centered in the block.

▼ *Enlarge x 200%*

PIECING THE QUILT TOP

4 Cut two pieces of 10¼ x 14¼ inches from the gingham fabric and two pieces of 8⅜ x 19¾ inches from the floral fabric. Make two side panels consisting of a bow block, floral block, and another bow block by stitching with edges and right sides together. Press seams open.

5 Make a third panel by stitching together the gingham blocks with the buggy block. Press seams open.

6 When all the panels are complete, assemble the quilt top by stitching, with edges and rights sides together, each of the side panels to the central buggy panel. Press seams open.

ASSEMBLING THE QUILT LAYERS

7 Cut a piece of batting and a piece of waterproof fabric 21⅛ x 37¾ inches. Place the waterproof fabric on the work surface, wrong side up and then place the batting on top of that. Finally place the completed quilt top, right side up onto the batting. Baste the layers together.

8 To quilt the layers together, stitch-in-the-ditch along the block seams using the ivory sewing thread.

9 To make the binding, cut two strips of black fabric on the bias, the width of your quilt top by 3¼ inches. Iron a ⅝-inch hem on both long sides of the binding strip and then press the strip in half along the length. Pin or baste it in place over the top and bottom edges of the quilt. Edge-stitch the binding in place with black thread and with the quilt top facing up. Be sure to catch the underside of the binding in the stitching.

10 Cut two more strips of black fabric 1¼ inches longer than the height of your quilt by 3¼-inches wide. Iron a ⅝-inch hem on both long sides of the binding strips and then press the strips in half lengthwise. Pin or baste it in place over the side edges of your quilt layers and the top and bottom binding. Tuck under the ends so the binding finishes the quilt edges neatly.

Edge-stitch the binding in place with black thread and the quilt top facing up. Be sure to catch the underside of the binding in the stitching.

11 Finish the quilt by embroidering pink French knots (see page 23 for technique) in the center of each of the rosettes on the bows.

Lace Diaper Hamper

DIFFICULTY
RATING: ✶ ✶

18 inches high

This hamper is handy for storing clean diapers above a changing table. The antique lace pattern has a modern look in its combinations of gingham and black and white designs.

The hanger width is 12 inches, which is narrower than most adult clothes hangers. Use a children's clothes hanger or saw the ends off a wooden one or bend a wire hanger to fit the shape. These instructions explain how to make your own bias binding, but you can buy double-fold bias binding in a matching color.

Materials

- ½ yard of cream cotton fabric
- Image transfer fluid
- ½ yard of pink cotton fabric
- Cream thread
- ¼ yard of black and white gingham fabric
- Scrap of black cotton fabric
- Scrap of pink felt
- 1 black button
- A piece of cardboard 11 x 17 inches
- A narrow hanger

Instructions

Note: All seam allowances are ⅝ inch unless otherwise stated.

THE LACE FRONT

1 To transfer the lace pattern onto the front of the hamper, enlarge the design on page 46 on a photocopier so it fills the length of an 11 x 17-inch sheet of paper. Make two photocopies and cut them out carefully, leaving very little white paper around the edges.

2 Cut a rectangle 16 x 32½ inches from the cream fabric and mark the center back at top and bottom, and the box pleats as shown in the diagram on page 124.

3 Spread the fabric out on a work surface with the right side up. Apply the lace pattern to the fabric with the image transfer fluid, ⅞ inch in and parallel to the shorter edges of the rectangle.

4 To make the binding for the front opening, cut two strips 2 x 16 inches across the bias of the pink fabric. Press a ⅜-inch hem along both sides and fold in half lengthwise, then press again. Pin the binding over the seam allowance of the hamper front so it butts up against the edge of the lace pattern. With the right side up, edge-stitch in place. Be sure to catch the underside of the bias binding in the machine stitching.

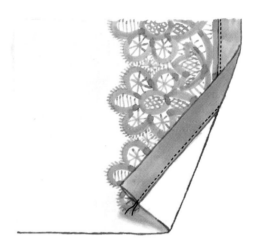

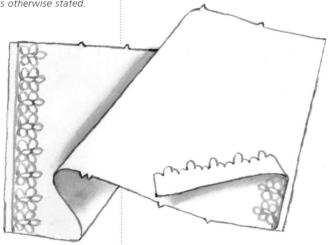

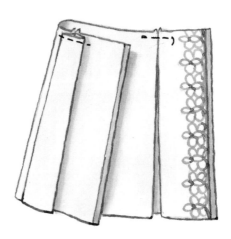

THE HANGER SLEEVE

5 To make the hanger sleeve, cut two pieces of the sleeve pattern from the gingham fabric. Put right sides together and stitch around the curved edge leaving a small gap in the middle for the hook of the hanger; leave the straight edge open. Clip seams, turn right side out and press.

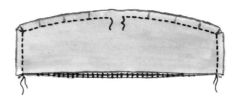

ATTACHING THE LACE FRONT TO THE HANGER SLEEVE

6 Make the two box pleats at the upper edge of the lace front by bringing the outside pleat markings together at the central pleat marking. Baste in place. With edges and wrong sides together, pin the lace front to the hanger sleeve with the bias bindings meeting at the center front and matching the notches in the center back; sew together. Trim the seam to ⅛ inch and press the seam upward.

7 To make the binding, first cut a 2 x 26-inch length of pink fabric across the bias. Press under ⅜ inch on each side of the bias strip and then fold it in half lengthwise and press again. Pin the bias binding over the seam, starting at the center front and continuing around until you reach center front again. Overlap the beginning of the binding slightly and trim off any extra (the open end of the binding will be hidden by the ribbon rosette). Stitch it in place, with the lace front facing up and the hanger sleeve tucked inside it. Be sure to catch in the underside of the binding. Turn the hanger sleeve right side out and press the binding up.

▲ *Lace Pattern*

MAKING THE ROSETTE

8 To make the rosette, cut a large circle from black fabric, a medium one from cream fabric, and a small one from pink felt using the templates provided on page 124. Using a long setting, stitch all around the edge of the black circle. Pull the bobbin thread to gather the puff as much as possible, then tie to secure. Spread the gathering stitch out evenly and press the puff flat.

9 Repeat step 8 with the cream circle. Place the cream disk on top of the black one with the gathered sides up and baste in place. Place the felt disk over the center of the cream rosette to hide the raw edge, and baste in place. Sew a black button on top.

10 The ribbon is made up of two 2½ x 18-inch bias strips of pink fabric. These are sewn with edges and right sides together, leaving a 4-inch gap in the middle so the ribbon can be turned right side out. Once the ribbon has been turned, press and baste it into a bow shape on the wrong side of the rosette.

MAKING THE HAMPER BASE

11 Cut two pieces of cream fabric for the hamper base using the pattern pieces on page 124. Mark the center front and back. With right sides together, pin the center back of one of the base pieces to the center back of the hamper. Continue pinning until you come to the corners of the base. Place your pins diagonally at the corners and clip diagonally into the hamper fabric almost up to the seam allowance. Continue pinning until the fronts of the hamper are in place (they do not meet in the middle). Baste in place along the seam allowance and then machine stitch. Turn right side out, trim seam allowance and corner, and press seams toward the base.

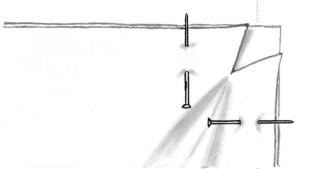

12 The second piece of base fabric will be the lining; press under all the seam allowances. Place the cardboard on top of the hamper base and then slipstitch the lining in place over it.

▼ *The decorative rosette in the center of the hamper.*

Three Little Ducks Sleeping Bag

DIFFICULTY
RATING: ✳ ✳ ✳

To fit baby up to 6 months

Sleeping bags prevent kicking babies from losing their covers at night. Line the sleeping bag with polar fleece or flannel if you want it to be warm and cozy, or use plain cotton for a warmer weather bag. To wash the bag, turn it inside out and use the temperature recommended by the manufacturer of the fusible bonding web.

Materials

- Assortment of bright-colored cotton scraps for back and front of sleeping bag
- ¼ yard of fusible bonding web
- Assortment of plain and patterned cotton scraps for appliqué
- Assortment of embroidery and sewing threads
- ¾ yard of cotton, flannel, or polar fleece fabric for bag lining
- 1 packet of 1-inch wide, double-fold bias binding in lavender
- 11-inch nylon zipper

Instructions

Note: All seam allowances are ⅝ inch unless otherwise stated.

ASSEMBLING FRONT AND BACK

1 Join an assortment of rectangular patterned and plain cotton fabrics together until you have two large rectangles, each measuring 19½ x 23½ inches. Make sure you have at least three plain patches large enough to fit the duck appliqués on the front piece. Cut out the sleeping bag backs and fronts using the pattern pieces on page 123.

APPLIQUÉ AND EMBROIDERY

2 Enlarge the templates below by 200% and trace them on the double-sided fusing, making sure you have enough pieces for two small and one large duck. Fuse these to the scraps of colored cotton and cut out. Compose three ducks on plain areas of the sleeping bag front and fuse them in place.

3 Use a combination of machine and embroidery stitches to secure and decorate the appliqué pieces. Decorate the plain areas with simple embroidery stitches such as French knots and running stitch (see pages 22–23 for techniques). Decorate the back of the sleeping bag in the same way or leave it plain.

ASSEMBLING THE SLEEPING BAG

4 With right sides together, stitch front shoulder seams to back shoulder seams. Stitch under the arms and around the bag bottom. Clip the corners and curves so that the fabric lies flat. Turn bag right side out and slash down the center front to the mark indicated on the front pattern piece.

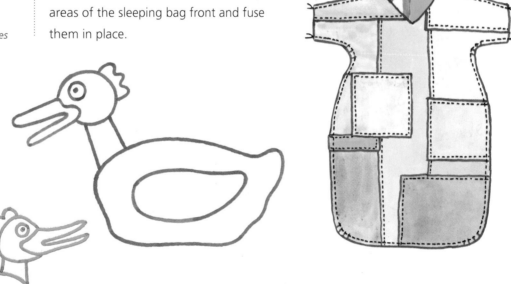

5 Cut one front and one back from lining fabric and sew together in the same way as the patched front and back, but do not turn right side out. Slash down the center front to the mark indicated on the front pattern piece.

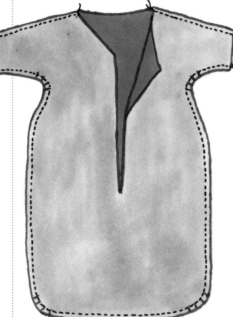

▼ *Add ties to the sides, securing them at the back, to fit the bag more closely to your baby.*

6 Put the lining inside the sleeping bag, wrong sides and raw edges together. Baste the neckline together down to the center front slash. Baste the sleeve holes together in the same way.

7 Cut a length of bias binding ½ inch longer than needed to go around neck and front opening. Fold the binding in half lengthwise and press. Starting at the center back, baste the binding over the raw edges of the neck and front opening. Continue basting until you reach the center back again and fold under the end of the binding for a neat finish.

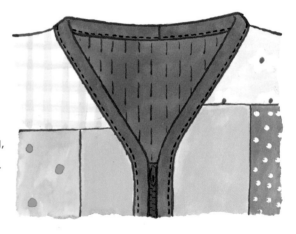

8 Baste the zipper in place so the bias binding overlaps it. Using a zipper foot, machine stitch all around the neck and center front, close to the edge of the bias binding. (See page 17 for sewing a zipper.)

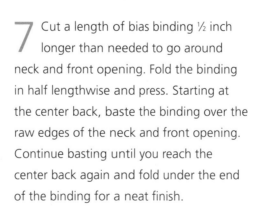

9 Cut two lengths of bias binding ½ inch longer than needed to go around the sleeve opening. Fold the bindings in half lengthwise and press. Starting at the underside of the sleeve, baste the binding over the raw edge of sleeve opening, turning under the ends. Machine stitch close to the edge of the bias binding. Remove all basting stitches.

Little Bird Purse

DIFFICULTY
RATING: ★ ★ ★

This project is perfect for using up small scraps of favorite fabrics and favorite buttons, as well as for testing different appliqué combinations. It can be used to store a baby's keepsakes or as a purse for a toddler.

Materials

- ¼ yard or scraps of fusible bonding web
- Scraps of cotton in about 6 different colors and patterns. If you choose patterned fabric, make sure the print is small.
- Embroidery and sewing threads
- 7 white buttons
- ¼ yard of cotton fabric for bag strap and piping
- 8½-inch nylon zipper
- ¼ yard of lining fabric

Instructions

Note: All seam allowances are ⅜ inch unless otherwise stated.

MAKING THE APPLIQUÉ FRONT

1 Trace the bird appliqué templates on the fusible bonding web and iron them to your selected fabrics. Cut each piece out and assemble the bird on a backing fabric that is larger than the size of the bag front.

2 A variety of stitches are used to secure the appliqué pieces. Running stitch in contrasting embroidery thread is used for the body and wing, a straight machine stitch outlines the feet, while a machine zigzag stitch holds the beak, head, and inner wing in place. French knots (see page 23) in cream embroidery thread are used to make the bird's eye, collar decoration, and tail spots.

3 Trace the outline of the bag front (see templates, on page 121) on the backing fabric and then embroider French knots and secure buttons around the bird within the seam allowance.

MAKING THE BAG

4 Using the templates on page 121, cut one each of the bag front, back, top, and bottom from both the bag and lining fabrics. For the length of piping cut two 1¼ x 18½-inch strips of fabric across the bias and for the strap cut a strip of fabric, parallel to the grain, 1½ x 36 inches.

5 To make the strap, turn under ⅜ inch on each long edge of the strip and press. Fold the strip in half lengthwise and press again. Edge-stitch in a matching thread. Baste the ends of the strap to the double notch seam allowance of the purse bottom, being sure to keep the strap from twisting as you work.

6 Fold the piping in half lengthwise and press. With edges and right sides together, baste one length of piping to the bag front and the other to the bag back, concealing the end by folding it under.

8 Press the seam allowance under on one of the long edges of each of the bag tops. Baste the zipper in place and then edge-stitch.

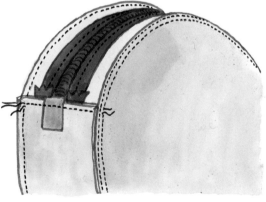

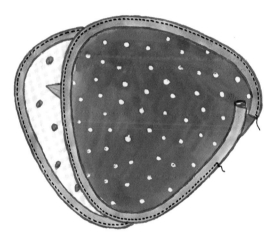

9 With the purse inside out and right sides together, sew the bag top to the front and then the back. Then sew across the bag side seams, including the zipper and strap ends in the stitching. Clip and trim the bag seam allowances around the curved edges.

7 With edges and right sides together, stitch the bag bottom to the bag front, leaving the seam allowance open above the notches. Sew the other side of the bag bottom to the bag back. Clip and trim the bag seam allowances around the curved edges.

▼ *The pearl white buttons add spots of light to this jolly little purse.*

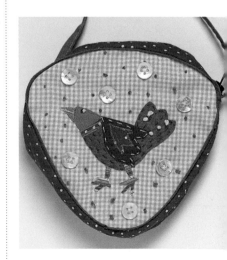

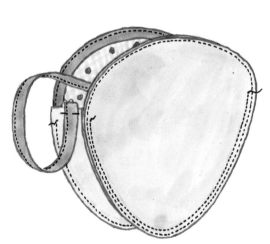

10 Make the lining in the same way, omitting the strap, piping, and zipper. With wrong sides together, slipstitch the lining in place over the zipper seam. Turn the purse right side out.

Monogrammed Linen Quilt

DIFFICULTY
RATING: ★

Size depends on your linen piece but at least 14 inches square to tuck around a newborn baby.

This quilt is made from an antique embroidered table linen that has been personalized with an appliquéed monogram letter. If the linen already has a lot of embroidery or printing, you may not wish to embellish it any further. The invisible fusing will hold the quilt layers together, making it unnecessary to quilt.

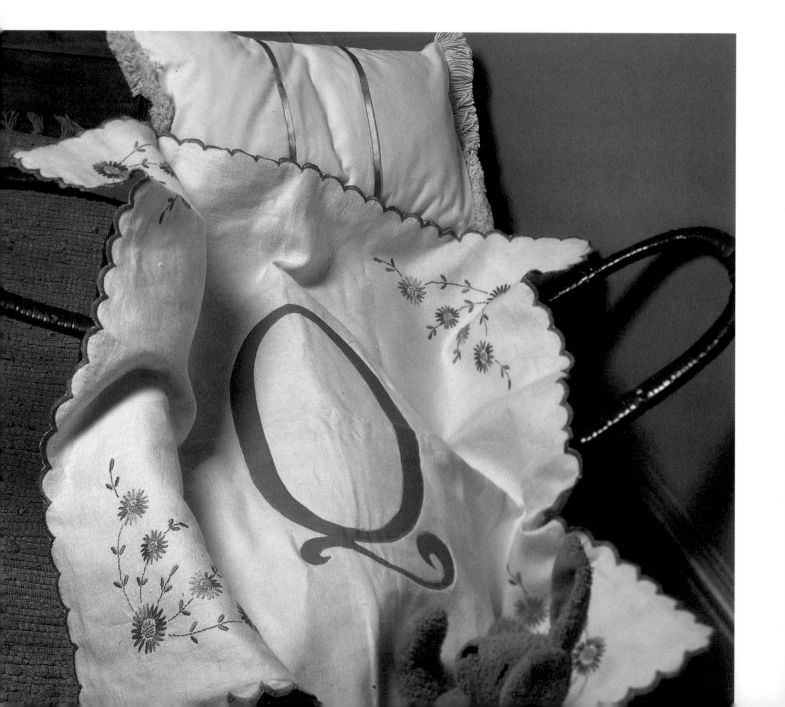

Materials

- *Vintage cloth of at least 14 inches square*
- *Backing fabric 3 inches larger than the vintage cloth*
- *100% cotton batting the same size as your vintage cloth*
- *¼ yard of colored cotton for monogram appliqué*
- *Fusible bonding web the size of your quilt backing plus ¼ yard for the monogram*
- *Sewing threads to match your vintage cloth and your appliqué fabric*

Instructions

Note: All seam allowances are ⅝ inch unless otherwise stated.

CUTTING THE QUILT BACKING AND BATTING

1 A feature of this embroidered table linen is its scalloped edge. Many vintage cloths may include pretty embroidery or lace around the edge that you can incorporate in the design. To do this construct the batting and backing of the quilt so that they are smaller than the quilt top.

When you have selected the quilt top fabric, gently press it and measure the length and width, excluding any lace or embroidered borders that you want to overhang the quilt. Cut the backing fabric 3 inches larger all the way around. Cut the cotton batting ⅜ inch smaller than the quilt top.

DECORATING THE QUILT TOP

2 To make an appliquéed monogram find an appropriate alphabet design. You might like to select one designed in the same period as your antique linen. Enlarge the letter or monogram design on a photocopier to fill the center of your quilt top. Cut out the letter and trace on cardboard to make a template.

3 Trace the letter template, wrong side up, onto your fusible bonding and then attach the fusing to the appliqué fabric. Cut out the appliqué and peel off the fusing paper. Carefully position your initial or monogram in the center of the quilt and press in place. Use a matching thread to zigzag or satin stitch the appliqué in place.

ATTACHING THE BATTING TO THE QUILT BACKING

4 Cut the fusible bonding web to the same size as the quilt batting. If the invisible fusing is narrower than the width of the batting, cut two pieces the length of the quilt and then trim the width until they are the same size as the batting. Iron both pieces of fusing to the batting, following the manufacturer's directions. Position the batting, adhesive side down, in the middle of the quilt backing to leave 3⅓ inches of quilt backing around all the outer edges. Fuse the batting to the backing.

ASSEMBLING THE QUILT LAYERS

5 Fold the 3⅓-inch hem of the quilt backing over the batting, keeping the corners square. Baste in place. With the batting side up on your work surface, lay the quilt top on the backing, concealing it completely. Baste the quilt layers together (see page 27 for technique). Slipstitch the backing to the quilt top.

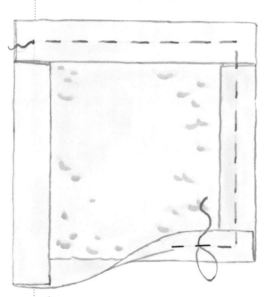

▼ *The decorative scalloped edge hides the outline of the backing and falls softly over the thickness of the quilt.*

QUILTING

6 It is not necessary to quilt the layers since the invisible fusing will hold the batting in place. However, you may like to tie it (see page 29 for technique) at intervals or machine stitch in straight or wavy lines to give it a quilted finish.

Our quilt has been machine-quilted using stitch-in-the-ditch around the outside of the appliquéed letter. Using the same thread as was used to zigzag the letter and a bobbin thread to match your backing fabric, machine stitch around the letter using a small straight stitch.

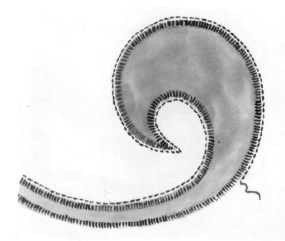

Vintage Pillows

DIFFICULTY
RATING: ★

6 x 12 inches

Old linen towels, hankies, scarves, aprons, and other vintage fabrics make perfect pillow covers. An abundance of these articles can be found cheaply at flea markets.

Our pillows are made from brightly printed linen towels. The unusual shape makes a good support for a mother feeding her baby as well as for propping up an infant learning to sit.

Materials

- *Vintage linen towels*
- *Machine-washable fabric for making the pillow casings (twice the size of each towel)*
- *Sewing thread*
- *Machine-washable stuffing*
- *Cotton backing fabric (one and a half times the size of each towel)*
- *Cotton fringe or other trimming*

Instructions

Note: All seam allowances are ⅝ inch unless otherwise stated.

MAKING THE PILLOW FORM

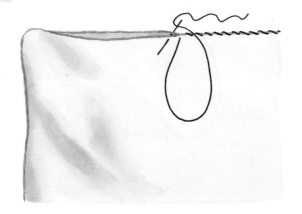

1 Each pillow has an inner form and a cover that can be taken off and washed separately. To make the pillow form, cut two pieces from casing fabric ⅜ inch smaller than your vintage cloth plus seam allowance. With right sides together, stitch around three sides of the pillow casing.

2 Turn casing right side out and stuff the pillow form. If you want a very firm pillow, pack as much stuffing into the casing as possible. Slipstitch the last seam together, turning under the seam allowance as you go.

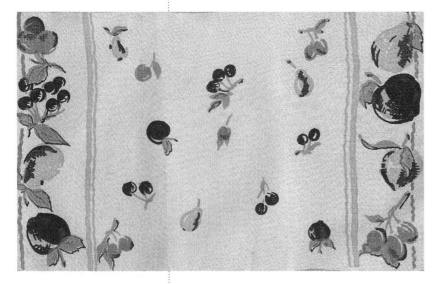

The size and design on the linen towels used here fit perfectly with the shape of a small pillow. However, if you have a selection of odd linen scraps that go together, you can easily join them to create an interesting patchwork effect, making the same rectangular shape used for the project shown here.

MAKING THE PILLOW COVER

3 Cut two pieces of the backing fabric, each an equal height and two-thirds the width of the vintage towel. These pieces will overlap at the center of the pillow back to create an envelope opening; this avoids any fasteners that could be dangerous to small children. To create the envelope opening, machine hem and press along the edge equal to the height of each piece. Then baste the envelope backings together, with the wrong side of one half overlapping the right side of the other half along the hemmed edges, giving you a pillow back that is the same size as your vintage towel.

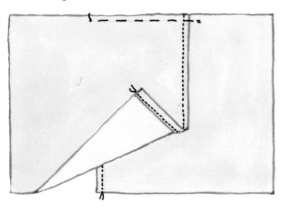

ADDING THE TRIMMING

4 Cut two pieces of trimming the same length as the pillow ends. With edges and right sides together, baste them to the backing material.

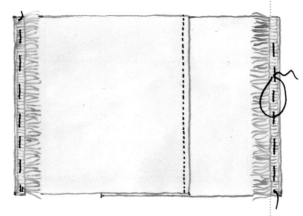

5 The trim will be sandwiched between the right sides of the backing and the pillow top when you machine stitch them together. Be sure to keep the trimming away from the side seam stitching; if necessary, use masking tape to hold it out of the way. With right sides together, stitch along all four sides. Press the seams and then turn the pillow cover right side out through the envelope opening. Press gently. Stuff the pillow form into the cover.

▼ *The cotton fringe complements the fabric on the cushions and because it is so soft, it makes an ideal trimming for a child's pillow.*

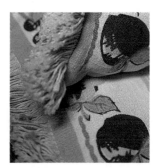

crib
quilts

These projects will be treasured as keepsakes. The quilts

are a good size for a standard crib but you may wish to

enlarge them so that they can be used on a larger bed.

Instructions for doing this are included with each project.

Humpty-Dumpty Quilt

DIFFICULTY
RATING: ✶ ✶

35 x 45 inches

Humpty-Dumpty falls off the bottom of this bright quilt for small children. The polka dots on the ground fabric are felt appliqués that are held in place with a simple French knot. The decorative running stitch around the dots quilts the layers together.

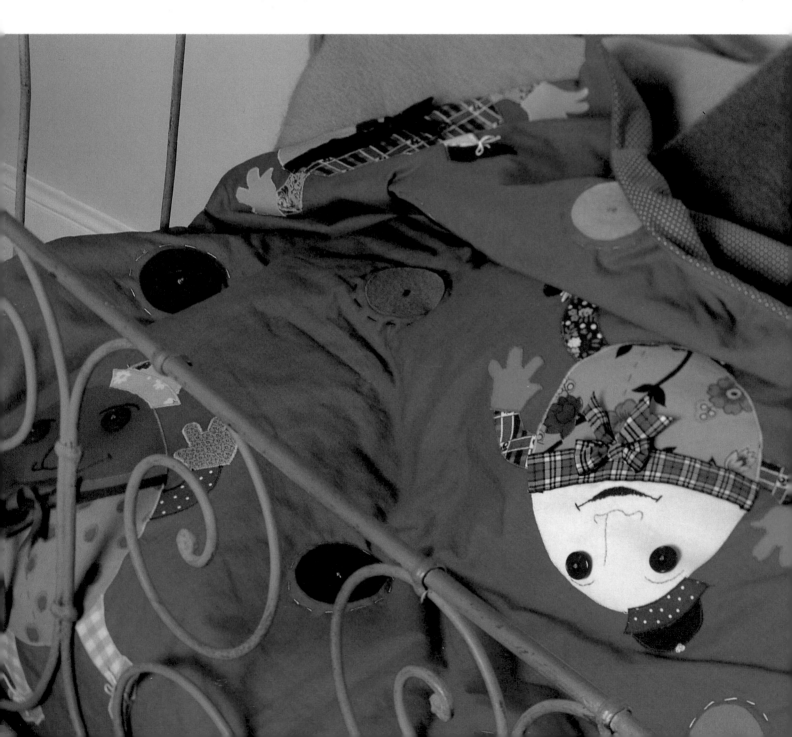

Materials

- *1 yard of turquoise background fabric*
- *½ yard of fusible bonding web*
- *Scraps of bright-colored and printed fabrics for appliqué*
- *Sewing threads to match appliqué fabrics*
- *Pencil*
- *8 buttons, ¾ inch in diameter.*
- *Selection of embroidery threads (floss)*
- *½ yard each of five different 1-inch wide ribbons*
- *1 yard of batting*
- *1 yard of green cotton lining fabric*
- *One craft square each of purple, lilac, blue, grass green, and sea green felt*

Instructions

Note: All seam allowances are ⅝ inch unless otherwise stated.

MAKING THE QUILT TOP

1 Cut a rectangle of turquoise cotton 36½ x 46½ inches.

2 Make five photocopies of the Humpty-Dumpty template on page 64. Cut out each copy and use the diagram below as a guide to placing them on the quilt. Trace the outlines lightly on the background fabric. Make sure that you reverse the template before tracing the outlines of the appliqué pieces on the fusible bonding web.

3 Iron the bonding pieces to the wrong sides of the appliqué fabrics and cut each one out.

4 Arrange the appliqué pieces on the quilt top following the pencil markings and iron in place following the manufacturer's directions. Zigzag each piece to the quilt top using thread to match the appliqué fabric.

5 Using the template as a guide, draw the mouth, nose, and eyebrows on Humpty-Dumpty's faces with a pencil. Use a fabric eraser to correct any mistakes. Backstitch the features with colored embroidery floss.

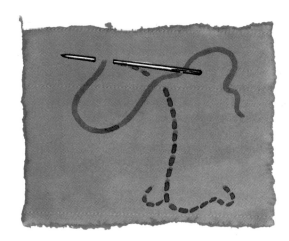

6 Sew the buttons in place for the eyes, or for a baby or toddler make the eyes with decorative embroidery stitches. Decorate the shoes with bows made from embroidery floss.

7 Cut the ribbons ¾ inch longer than Humpty-Dumpty's neck length, and baste them in place, turning under the ends. Make a bow with the remaining ribbon and secure it in the middle of the ribbon.

9 Trace 20 polka dots, using the template on page 121, on fusible bonding web and iron four polka dots to each of the felt fabrics. Cut them out. Place the polka dots on the quilt top arranging them evenly over the area around the Humpty-Dumpty figures.

10 Use a French knot (see page 23) in contrasting embroidery thread to secure each dot. To finish, outline each dot in running stitch to quilt the layers together. Repeat this stitch running from the base of Humpty-Dumpty's bow to the base of the body.

▲ *Use bold patterned fabric to dress Humpty-Dumpty.*

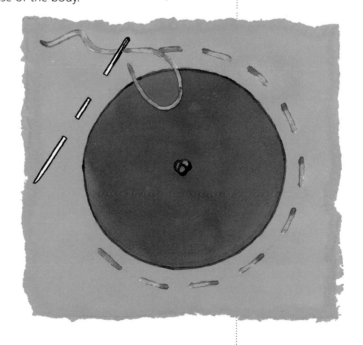

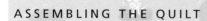

ASSEMBLING THE QUILT

8 Cut the quilt back and batting 36½ x 46½ inches. Follow the directions for bagging out a quilt in the techniques section on page 27.

Humpty-Dumpty Sweatshirt

This appliqué design fits on a toddler's sweatshirt or jacket back. It can also be reduced on a photocopier to make a smaller appliqué for baby clothes. All the stitching is done by hand, making it an excellent portable project.

Materials

- *Scraps of bright-colored and printed cotton fabrics*
- *¼ yard of fusible bonding web*
- *One cotton sweatshirt*
- *Variety of embroidery and sewing threads*
- *Pencil*
- *2 red buttons*
- *½ yard of ½-inch wide plaid ribbon*

1 Using the Humpty-Dumpty template, trace all the appliqué pieces on the fusible bonding web. Iron the fusing to the wrong side of the appliqué fabrics and carefully cut out.

2 Arrange the appliqué pieces on the sweatshirt and iron in place following the manufacturer's directions. Slipstitch the edges of the appliqué to the sweatshirt.

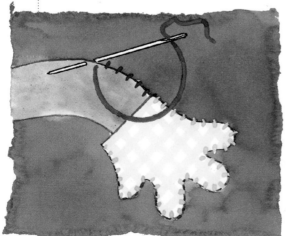

3 Using the template as a guide, draw the mouth, nose, and eyebrows on Humpty-Dumpty's face. Use a fabric eraser to correct any mistakes. Backstitch with colored embroidery floss.

4 Sew the buttons in place for the eyes. Decorate his hat with French knots and his shoes with bows made from embroidery floss.

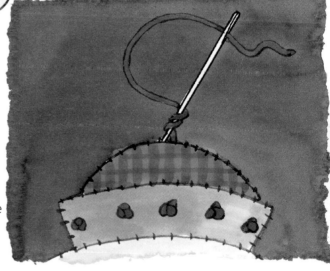

5 Cut the ribbon ¾ inch longer than Humpty-Dumpty's neck length and baste it in place, turning under the ends. Make a bow with the remaining ribbon length and secure it to the middle of the ribbon at his neck.

"All About Me" Quilt

DIFFICULTY
RATING: ★ ★

39 x 44 inches

This quilt works equally well as a bed quilt or a wall hanging. It includes hand prints made with fabric paints and a fantasy portrait.

The portrait is made by transfering a photo of your child's face to an appliquéed body. Templates are included of a child in a dress or pants. The templates of a child in an airplane, used in the next project, can also be used if they are scaled up large enough to fill a rectangle 12 x 17 inches.

Materials

- ½ yard of cream cotton fabric
- White, blue, and pink fabric paints and a color to match your child's skin
- 1 yard of blue polka dot cotton fabric
- Color photograph of child
- Image transfer fluid
- ⅛ yard of fusible bonding web
- Scraps of colored and printed cotton fabrics for appliqué, some to match child's skin tone
- ¼ yard of turquoise cotton fabric
- ¼ yard of salmon pink fabric
- Assortment of embroidery and sewing threads
- Trims for decorating appliqué
- ½ yard of hot pink cotton fabric
- ½ yard of pink gingham fabric
- ¼ yard of blue floral fabric
- ⅛ yard of purple cotton fabric
- ⅛ yard of purple-blue cotton fabric
- 1 yard of hot pink backing fabric
- 1 yard of batting

MAKING THE HAND PRINTS

1 Cut ten 8-inch squares of fabric from the cream-colored cotton. This quilt only uses four but you will want extras to allow for mistakes and experiments.

2 Prepare the printing area by taping a plastic bag to the table. Mix four different colors of paint on the paper plates; allow about one tablespoon of paint for every 2-3 hand prints. You will need a separate sponge to apply each color to the child's hand. Make sure your child is wearing an apron or an old shirt and that there are plenty of paper towels on hand for cleaning between prints.

3 Sponge a little paint on the child's hand and ask her or him to do a test print by pressing down on newsprint. Apply the paint again and press down in the center of the fabric square. Apply fresh paint for each print, cleaning hands with paper towels between colors. Let the prints dry and set the fabric paints with an iron according to the manufacturer's directions.

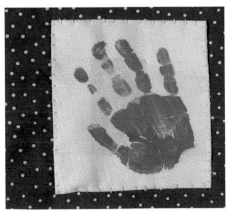

4 When the hand prints are finished, trim the squares, baste the edges under, and press.

MAKING THE FANTASY PORTRAIT

5 Cut a rectangle of fabric 13½ x 18½ inches for your portrait background. Enlarge one of the appliqué templates on page 70 by 200% on a photocopier and cut it out. Holding the template upside-down, trace it on your portrait background fabric so you know where to place the image transfer and appliqué pieces.

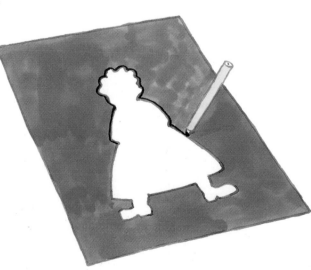

6 Select a photograph of your child that is evenly lit and well exposed. Photographs made in photo booths are good for this purpose. Calculate the amount that you will need to enlarge this photograph for it to fit into the template head (see page 25 for technique) and enlarge the photograph on a color copier. Carefully cut out your child's head from the photocopy and apply it to your background fabric following the image transfer fluid directions (on page 25). You may need to paint the head area first, with paint appropriate to your child's skin tone in order for the image to stand out.

7 Trace the template pieces on fusible bonding web and fuse them to the appliqué fabrics. Choose a cotton fabric that is close to your child's skin tone for the neck and hands. Fuse the appliqué pieces in place, being careful not to touch the image transfer with the iron.

8 Use decorative stitches to hold appliqué pieces in place. Add trims such as lace, ribbons, buttons, and beads. The child in our quilt holds a purchased ribbon rose; the leaves and stem are made by satin-stitching by hand. Your child could be holding a wand with an appliquéed star, a baseball bat, or a ball. You may want to touch up the photocopy or add details to the costume with fabric paint.

9 Baste the edges of the rectangle under and press.

MAKING THE QUILT TOP

The quilt top is made by piecing various-sized fabric rectangles together in an arrangement that balances the appliqués.

10 Begin by cutting a 35½-inch square from blue polka-dot cotton, an 11¾ x 14¼-inch rectangle from hot pink cotton fabric, and an 11¾ x 17¾-inch rectangle from pink gingham. With edges and right sides together, stitch the rectangles together along their shorter sides. Press seam open. With edges and right sides together, stitch the pieced rectangles to the blue polka-dot square, following the diagram. Press seam open.

Tools and Equipment

- *One large sponge cut into 4 smaller pieces*
- *Four paper plates*
- *Plastic bag*
- *Tape*
- *Paper towels*

Instructions

Note: All seam allowances are ⅝ inch unless otherwise stated.

11 Cut a strip of blue floral fabric 5½ x 21 inches and a strip of turquoise cotton 5½ x 26 inches and stitch them, edges and right sides together, along their shorter sides. Stitch this unit to the left side of the quilt, with right sides together. Press seams open.

12 Cut a strip of purple fabric 2½ x 40 inches and a strip of purple-blue fabric 2½ x 7 inches. Stitch these together along their short side and press seam open. Stitch this strip, right sides together, to the right side of the quilt. Press all seams open.

13 Place the appliqué hand squares and the portrait on the quilt as shown below and pin in place. Use a decorative stitch to hold the appliqués in place. Remove basting stitches. You may also want to decorate other quilt blocks with embroidery stitches or trimming.

ASSEMBLING THE QUILT

14 Cut the quilt back and batting to 41½ x 45½ inches. Follow the directions for bagging out a quilt in the techniques section on page 27. Tie the quilt layers every 4 inches, using cream-colored pearl cotton, and placing the bow on the backing side.

▲ *Brightly patterned fabrics make a simple design seem more complex.*

Portrait of a Pilot

DIFFICULTY
RATING: ★

9 x 9 inches

This fabric picture can be displayed in a box frame or held to the wall using self-adhesive hook-and-loop fastening. To personalize your portrait, consider using scraps of fabric or buttons from favorite old clothing belonging to the child.

If the picture hangs in a frame, it is safe to include such notions as plastic airplanes or other parts of small toys. Search your local dollar store for items to make your picture unique. These can be added using strong glue or hung from the bottom of the picture like fringe.

Materials

- Scraps of plain and printed cotton fabrics in an assortment of colors
- Sewing threads
- 9-inch square of quilt batting or felt
- 10½-inch square of lining fabric
- Pencil
- Well-lit matt photograph with a head and shoulder view of your child
- Image transfer fluid
- Fabric paints in white, red, blue, and yellow
- Scraps of fusible bonding web
- Decorative trims and notions such as ribbons, snaps, buttons, and pom-poms
- Metallic and cotton embroidery threads

Instructions

Note: All seam allowances are ⅝ inch unless otherwise stated.

MAKING THE GROUND FABRIC

1 Create a ground fabric by piecing together a variety of plain and printed cotton scraps into a 10½-inch square. Keep the ground design simple; you will have a chance to embellish it later with embroidery and appliqué. Baste under the ¾-inch hem allowance and press.

2 Cut a 9¾-inch square from the batting or felt and place it on the wrong side of the ground fabric. Baste it in place and trim it so it is not visible on the right side of the finished picture.

3 Cut a 10½-inch square of fabric for your lining and turn under the hem allowance. Overcast this to the wrong side of the picture fabric, sandwiching the hem allowances and batting between the ground fabric and lining.

TRANSFERING THE PHOTOCOPY

4 Make a black and white photocopy of the airplane template on page 75. Cut it out and holding it upside down, trace the outline of the airplane on your ground fabric with a pencil.

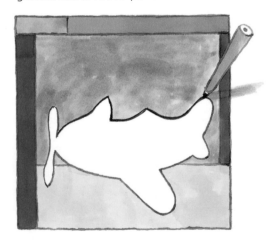

5 Enlarge or reduce the photo of your child on a color copier to fit inside the plane (see page 25 for technique).

6 Carefully cut out the head and shoulders of your photocopy and transfer them to the ground fabric following the instructions on page 24. Remember, you need to paint the transfer area white first if you are using a ground fabric that is not white or cream.

MAKING THE APPLIQUÉ AIRPLANE

7 Trace the template pieces on fusible bonding web and iron them to the wrong side of the appliqué fabrics. Fuse the appliqué pieces in place on your picture, being careful not to touch the image transfer with your iron.

8 Use decorative stitches to hold the appliqué pieces in place. Add trims such as lace, ribbons, buttons, and beads.

▲ *You may want to touch up the photocopy or add details to the picture with fabric paints.*

Animal Quilt

DIFFICULTY
RATING: ★ ★

35 x 45 inches

Toddlers will recognize the animals in this bright quilt. Amish colors, jewel tones, or graphic black, white, and gray would also make excellent combinations.

To make a quilt 50 x 70 inches for a single bed, use 9-inch patchwork squares and enlarge the templates 140% on a photocopier.

Materials

- *1 yard of ivory cotton*
- *¼ yard of seven different-colored cottons*
- *½ yard of fusible bonding web*
- *Selection of embroidery and sewing threads*
- *1 yard of cotton fabric for lining*
- *1 yard of batting*
- *5 yards of double-fold gingham binding*

Cutting guide for appliqué pieces

2 Foxes

3 Hens

2 Roosters

2 Rabbits

2 Hares

3 Cats

2 Dogs

3 Birds A

3 Birds B

2 Squirrels

1 Pig

6 Hearts

Instructions

Note: All seam allowances are ⅝ inch unless otherwise stated.

ASSEMBLING THE QUILT TOP

1 Cut 31 6-inch ivory squares. Cut five 6-inch squares from four of the colored cottons and four 6-inch squares from the remaining three colored cottons. You will now have a total of 63 colored and ivory squares.

2 Trace the appliqué templates on the fusible bonding web.

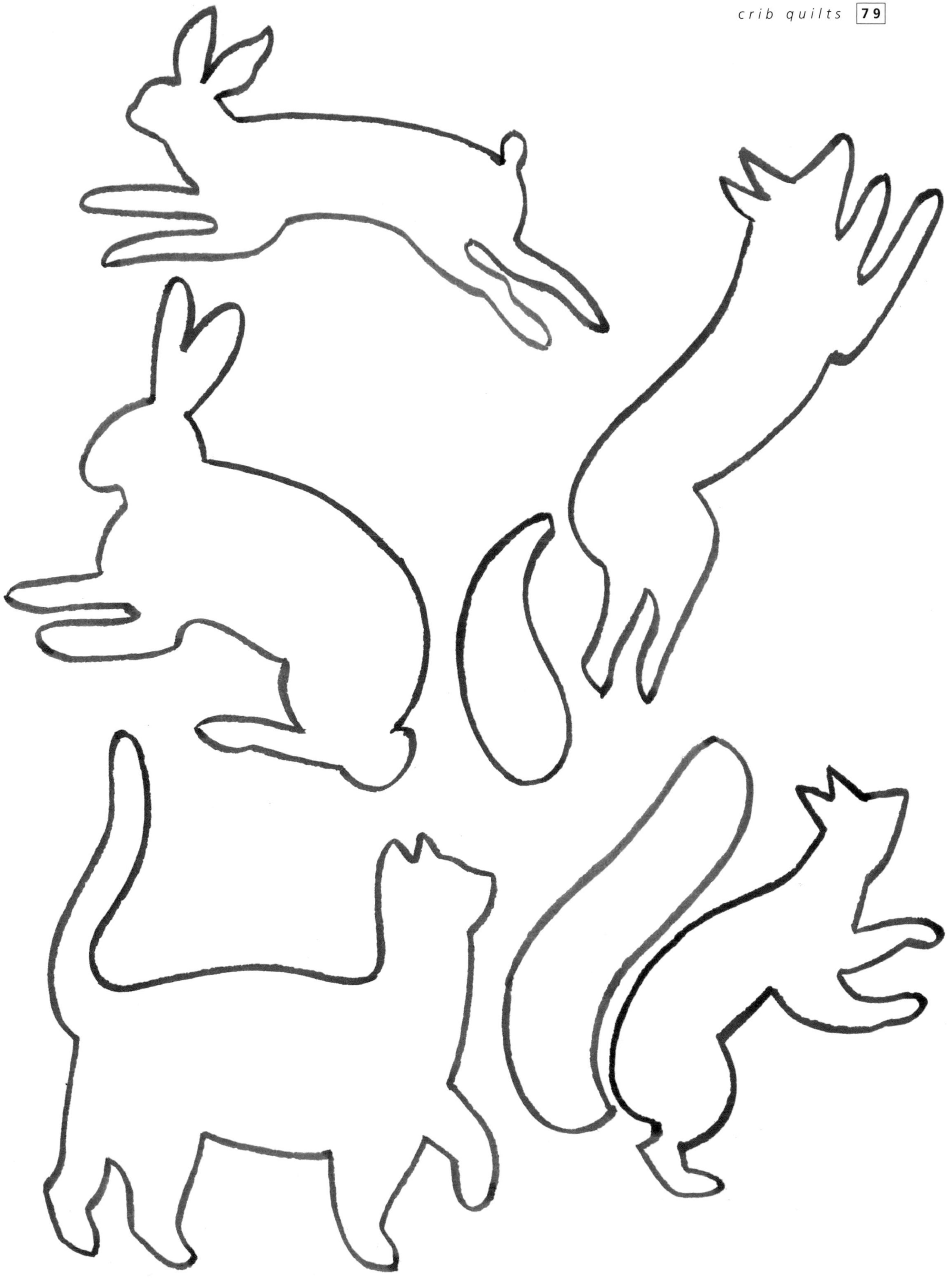

3 Iron web shapes to scraps of colored cottons, using the cutting guide as a guide to color and quantity of each appliqué piece.

4 Iron the appliqués to the ivory squares. Zigzag the edges of the appliqué pieces using matching thread.

5 Arrange the quilt blocks, and chain-piece vertical strips together (use the diagram below as a guide to placement). Press seams flat.

▼ *A close-up of the finished quilt.*

6 Sew the seven chained strips together, matching seams, to complete the quilt top. Press seams flat.

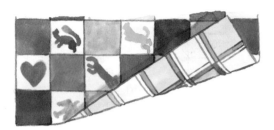

ASSEMBLING THE QUILT

7 Layer the quilt and baste together. Make a tie at the corner seam of each patch with the knot on the backing side of the quilt.

8 Bind edges of the quilt with the double-fold binding (see page 28 for technique). Remove all basting stitches.

Hearts Hat

DIFFICULTY
RATING: ★

To fit a child up to 18 months

This hat makes a great sun bonnet when it is lined with a light pink or blue gingham. It can be lined with polar fleece to make a warm winter hat.

Materials

- ¼ yard of six different-colored cotton fabrics
- ½ yard of gingham for hat lining
- Selection of embroidery and sewing threads
- Scraps of fusible bonding web for appliqué
- Tassel, button, or pompom for top of hat

Instructions

Note: All seam allowances are ¼ inch unless otherwise stated.

1 Using the pattern pieces on page 120, cut five crown sections and two brims (one for the lining) from different colored cottons. With edges and right sides together, sew each crown section to the next, leaving the bottom edge open. Press seams open.

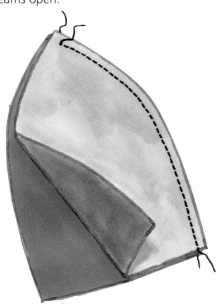

2 Trace the heart template on page 120 ten times on scraps of fusible bonding web. Iron the bonding hearts onto two different colors of cotton fabric, making five heart appliqués of each color. Carefully cut out each heart and fuse them to the hat brim, one under each point, ½ inch above the bottom edge. Zigzag around the outside of each heart appliqué using matching thread.

3 With edges and right sides together, sew the hat brim ends together. Press seam open. Repeat with the brim lining.

4 With edges and right sides together, sew the hat brim to its lining along the pointed edge. Clip and trim seam allowances. Turn brim right side out, carefully pushing the points out using a knitting needle or blunt scissors; press.

5 With edges together and brim lining next to the right side of the hat crown, sew around the lower edge of the hat. Press seam allowance under.

8 Machine stitch next to lining edge. Press brim up to conceal lining and stitching.

9 Stitch tassel, button, or pompom to the top of the hat crown. If you are making your own tassel, use a couple of different colored felts to complement the colors of the crown sections.

▲ *Felt has been used to make the decorative tassel on the top of the hat.*

6 Cut five crown sections from gingham and sew them together as in step 1. Press the seam allowance along the base to the wrong side.

7 With wrong sides together and seam allowances concealed, place the hat lining inside the hat and pin it in place so the lining hides the brim seam allowance.

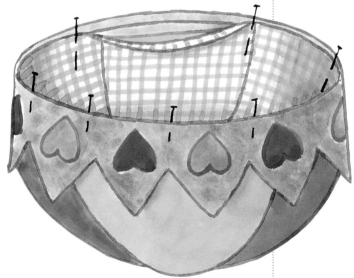

Space Rocket Quilt

DIFFICULTY
RATING: ★ ★

35 x 45 inches

This quilt is quick and versatile. The polar fleece makes it soft and warm without batting. The rocket's denim background is made from an old pair of adult jeans. The pocket in the top corner is part of the original jeans and a fun place to store a toy alien or other keepsake.

Materials

- *1 pair of adult jeans or 2-3 pairs of children's jeans*
- *Assortment of sewing and embroidery threads*
- *3½ yards of 1-inch wide double-fold pink binding*
- *½ yard of medium-weight interfacing*
- *1 yard of plaid polar fleece*
- *½ yard of fusible bonding web*
- *Scraps of colored cotton fabrics*
- *½ yard of plaid cotton fabric*
- *Trimming such as rickrack and ribbon*
- *Notions such as buttons, snaps, grippers, hooks and eyes, and star-shaped buttons*
- *5 yards of 1-inch wide double-fold purple binding*

Instructions

Note: All seam allowances are ⅝ inch unless otherwise stated.

MAKING THE DENIM BACKGROUND

1 Cut up the jeans and piece them to make a rectangle of fabric that measures 20 x 35 inches. Include a back pocket from the jeans in the upper right-hand corner.

2 Stitch the double-fold pink binding so that it encases the raw edge of the denim rectangle.

MAKING THE ROCKET APPLIQUÉ

3 Trace the outline of the rocket (see page 86) on the medium-weight interfacing and fuse it to the plaid fabric. Cut out the rocket leaving a ⅜-inch hem allowance.

4 Baste under the hem allowance and press.

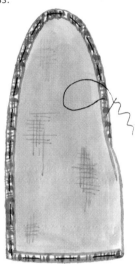

5 Trace the templates for the decoration of the rocket body (see page 86) on the fusible bonding web and iron them onto fabric scraps. Cut out the appliqués and iron them to the rocket. Decorate the rocket with trimmings, notions, and embroidery stitches.

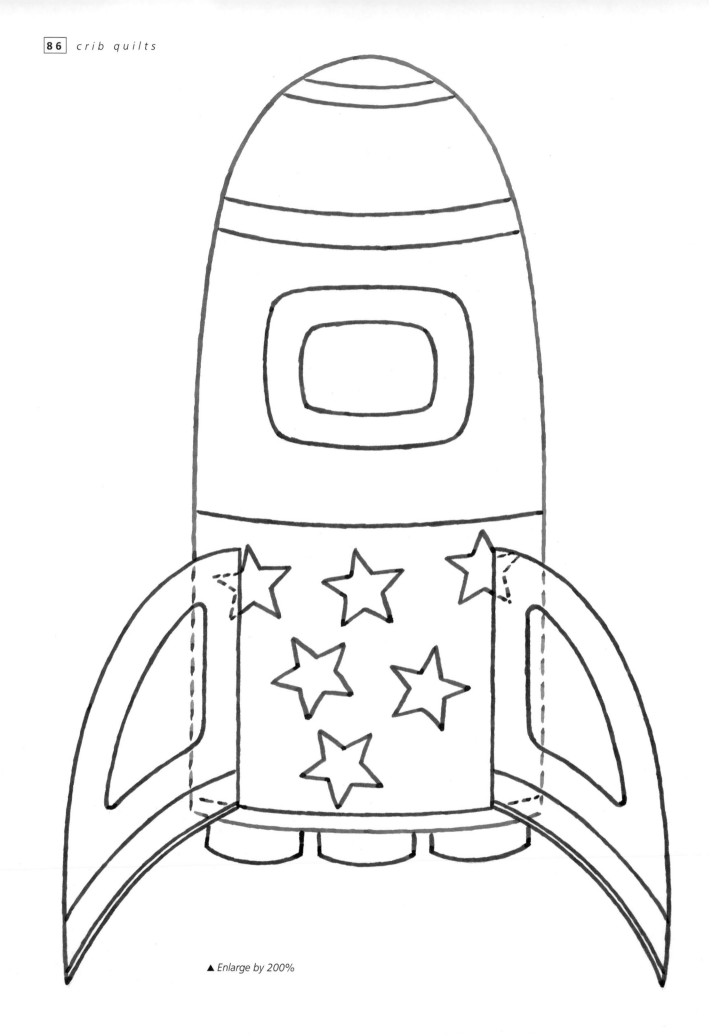

▲ *Enlarge by 200%*

6 Slipstitch the body of the rocket to the center of the denim rectangle.

7 Trace the three exhaust-pipe appliqués on the medium-weight interfacing and iron them to the wrong side of the exhaust pipe fabric. Cut out the pipes, leaving a ⅜-inch hem allowance. Baste under the seam allowance and slipstitch it to the denim fabric at the bottom of the rocket.

8 Trace the wing shapes on the interfacing and fuse them to the wrong side of the wing fabric. Cut out the wings, leaving a ⅜-inch hem allowance, and baste the seam allowance under. Trace the template pieces for the wing decoration on the bonding web and iron them on colored fabric scraps. Cut out and iron to the wings. Decorate the wings with trimmings, notions, and embroidery stitches. Slipstitch the wings in place.

9 Make the exhaust spots on the denim from French knots using embroidery floss (see page 23).

ASSEMBLING THE QUILT LAYERS

10 Cut a rectangle of 35 x 45 inches from the polar fleece and bind it with purple double-fold binding. Slipstitch the denim rectangle to the center of the polar fleece.

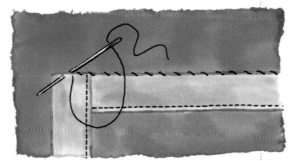

▼ *Make the space alien toys on page 88, to go with this quilt.*

Space Alien Toys

DIFFICULTY
RATING: *

These toys can easily be made from scraps. They are particularly cuddly made from polar fleece. The smaller alien fits inside the space rocket quilt pocket and the pocket of the big alien.

These toys have been decorated with small notions such as snaps and grippers; use embroidered decoration if you are making them for a baby or very small child.

SMALL ALIEN TOY

Materials

- *Scraps of three different fabrics*
- *Sewing thread*
- *Fiberfill*
- *1 small pompom*
- *1 pair of snaps*
- *Red embroidery thread*
- *5 inches of ½-inch wide ribbon*
- *1 star button*
- *2 hook closures*

Instructions

Note: All seam allowances are ¼ inch unless otherwise stated.

▲ *Use bright-colored threads and ribbons to decorate your alien toys.*

SMALL ALIEN TOY

1 Cut the small alien pattern pieces on page 125 from scraps of fabric. Join the head, top, and bottom pieces together for the front and the back of the alien, matching notches.

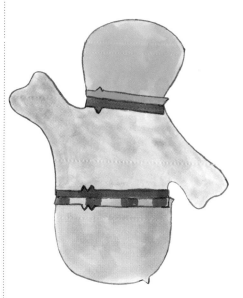

2 With right sides together, stitch around the body, leaving the seam open between notched dots. Turn the body right side out using the unsharpened end of a pencil to push the arms through. Stuff the alien with fiberfill and then slipstitch the alien closed, turning in the seam allowance.

3 Decorate the alien's top with red French knots. Sew a pompom to the center of his face for a nose, and attach snaps for eyes. Backstitch a smile with red embroidery thread. Wrap the ribbon around his neck and tack it in place, hiding the ends under a star-shaped button. Sew two hook closures to the top of his head for antennae.

LARGE ALIEN TOY

Materials

- *¼ yard of red polar fleece*
- *Scraps of blue and purple polar fleece*
- *Embroidery and sewing threads*
- *Batting*
- *4 inches of plaid polar fleece or flannel*
- *2 large snaps*
- *3 small pompoms*
- *½ yard of ribbon*

LARGE ALIEN TOY

1 Cut the large alien's body and arms, using the pattern pieces on page 125, from the red polar fleece. Cut ears, pocket, and base from scraps of blue and purple polar fleece. Assemble the ears by sewing two pieces together all the way around. Trim seam allowance very close to the seam. As this fabric does not fray, the ears do not need to be turned inside out. Baste ears to the top front of the alien's head, placing them toward the center of the body, edges and right sides together.

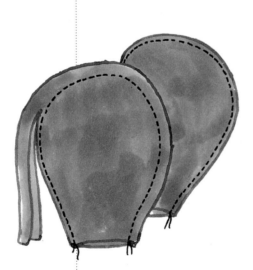

2 Assemble the hands by sewing around the outside, leaving the base open. Trim the seam allowance close to seam and stuff each hand with a little batting. Baste arms to the front of the body between notches, toward the center of the body, edges and right sides together.

3 With edges and right sides together, stitch the front of the body to the back. Turn right side out. Cut a strip of plaid fabric 3 x 16¼ inches. Stitch the short ends with right sides together. Match this seam to one on the side of alien's body and stitch the body to plaid fabric with edges and right sides together.

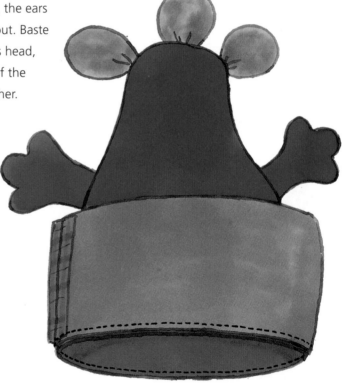

4 Turn the alien inside out again and with the right sides together, match the notch on the base to the side seam of plaid fabric and sew around the base, leaving 3½ inches open. Turn the alien right side out. Slipstitch the pocket in place, leaving top open.

6 Backstitch a mouth with embroidery thread. Satin-stitch a nose and attach snaps for eyes. Add a pompom to the center of the ears. Make a bow from the ribbon and tack to the center of the body.

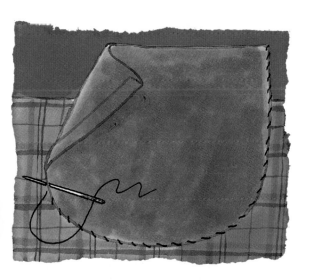

5 Fill the alien with batting and then attach the base. Slipstitch it to the plaid fabric, all the way round, making sure you turn in the seam allowance for a neat finish.

▲ *Place the toys at the end of the bed while your child is sleeping.*

single-bed
quilts

These projects are designed to grow with your child.

The bright colors make them suitable for small children

but the designs will survive into their teen years.

House, Hearts, and Stars Quilt

DIFFICULTY
RATING: ★ ★

60 x 95 inches

This single-bed quilt is one a child can grow up with, equally suitable for a toddler or a teenager. The house, hands, and hearts have a folk-art flavor.

To make a crib quilt of a similar design, reduce the number of central squares from 10 by 17 to 7 by 9 and include the same border. Redistribute the appliqué motifs.

Materials

- 1¾ yards of ivory cotton
- ½ yard each of 16 different-colored cottons
- 1 yard of fusible bonding web
- Sewing thread to match appliqué fabrics
- Scraps of colored fabrics for appliqué
- 3 yards of 45-inch wide cotton sheeting for quilt backing
- 3 yards of 45-inch wide batting
- Embroidery thread for tying quilt
- 9 yards of double-fold bias binding

Instructions

Note: All seam allowances are ⅜ inch unless otherwise stated.

MAKING THE CENTRAL PANEL

1 Using template A on page 126, cut out 27 squares from ivory cotton and 143 squares from the 16 different-colored cottons, to make a total of 170 squares.

2 Trace the templates shown here on the fusible bonding web and fuse them to the appliqué fabrics. Carefully cut out the appliqué pieces and iron them to the appropriate quilt patches. Refer to the diagram for quantity and placement of the appliqué pieces.

3 Zigzag around the appliqué shapes using matching thread.

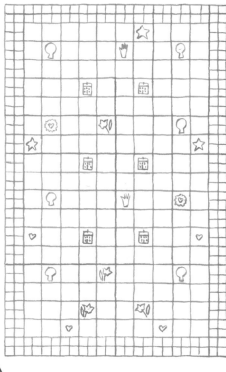

4 Place the quilt blocks on the floor in the desired arrangement, placing the colors in such a way as to create a checkered effect and referring to the diagram on page 95. Then sew the blocks together, edges and right sides together, in vertical strips of fifteen blocks. You will have ten strips. Iron seams open.

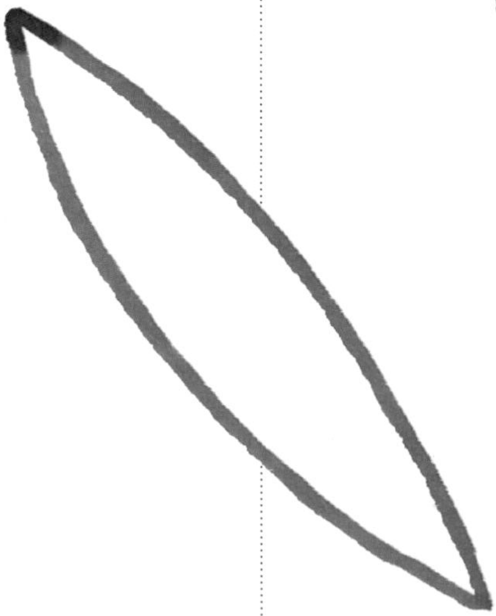

5 With edges and right sides together, sew the ten strips together in the right sequence to create the checkered effect and complete the central panel. Iron seams open.

MAKING THE BORDER

6 The border for this quilt is made of checkered white and colored squares. Using template B on page 126, cut 116 ivory and 116 colored squares of fabric.

7 Sew the squares together in four strips of 38 squares and four strips of 20 squares, alternating a colored square with an ivory one. Press all the seams open.

8 Sew the strips together, matching all seams, to make up two long checkered borders for the sides of quilt and two short borders for the top and bottom as in the diagram. Iron all seams open at the back of work.

9 With edges and right sides together, sew the top and bottom borders to the central panel of the quilt. Press seams open. Repeat for the side borders.

ASSEMBLING THE QUILT

10 Cut the quilt backing and batting to measure 60 x 95 inches. Baste the three layers of the quilt together (see page 24 for technique) and then trim the backing and batting to the same size as the quilt top.

11 Tie the quilt at corner seams, placing the knots at the back.

12 Bind the quilt with double-fold bias binding (see page 28 for technique) and remove all basting stitches.

▼ *A detail of the colorful motif on the quilt.*

Beanbag Seat

DIFFICULTY
RATING: ✱ ✱

16-inch diameter by 15-inch high

Beanbag chairs are great fun for children. This one is the perfect height for a child's stool or footrest. By lowering the height of this design, you can make an ideal seat for a smaller child. The more pellets in the seat, the firmer it will be. Ours is firmly stuffed, but it will become squashier with use.

Materials

- ¼ yard of fusible bonding web
- ½ yard each of four different-colored heavy cottons
- Sewing thread to match appliqué fabrics
- 15-inch nylon zipper
- 1 yard of nylon knit fabric
- 2-3 pounds of styrofoam pellets

Instructions

Note: All seam allowances are ⅝ inch unless otherwise stated.

MAKING THE PENDANTS

1 Using the template for the pendants on page 122, trace 20 triangles on the fusible bonding web. Iron equal numbers of these to four different fabrics. Carefully cut out the triangles and peel off the backing paper.

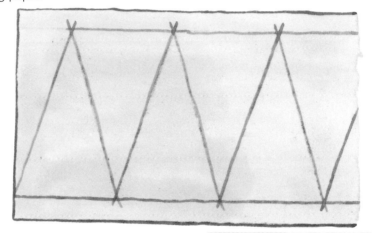

2 Iron the triangles onto matching fabrics so that each triangle is a single color, leaving a border of at least ¼ inch all around.

3 Zigzag around the two long edges of each triangle, leaving the short edge unstitched. Cut out the pendants close to the stitching.

MAKING THE POCKET

4 Repeat steps 1 and 2 for the pocket, using the template on page 122. Zigzag around the outside of the pocket.

5 Trace the star appliqué template on page 120 on fusible bonding web and iron it onto green fabric. Fuse the star to the middle of the pocket and zigzag around the shape.

ASSEMBLING THE SEAT COVER

6 Using the templates on page 120, cut two pieces for the seat base, one piece for the top and two pieces for the body from contrasting fabrics.

7 Insert the zipper into the center seam of the base between zipper markings (see page 17 for technique).

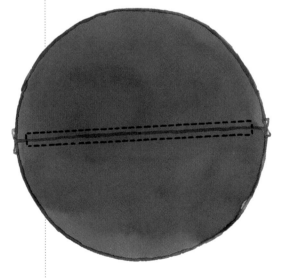

▲ *The contrasting pocket adds decoration, as well as being useful for storing books, pens or small toys.*

8 Matching the 16-inch sides of the seat body pieces, sew with edges and right sides together. Press seam open.

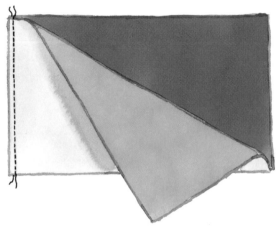

9 On the right side, place the pocket so it is centered over the seat body seam. Pin the pocket side seams parallel to one another with the pocket pouch out. Edge-stitch around the pocket, leaving the top open.

10 With edges and right sides together, sew the back seat body seams together to make a tube. Press the seam open.

11 Pin all the pendant triangles to the seat top at equal distances, with edges and right sides together. Machine baste the triangles in place.

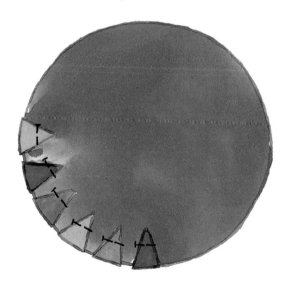

12 Pin and stitch the seat top to the body with edges and right sides together. Pin and stitch the seat base to the body with edges and right sides together, leaving zipper open. Clip the seam allowances and turn the bag right side out.

MAKING THE BEAN BAG

13 Cut two seat tops and two seat bodies from nylon knit fabric. Sew the body pieces together to make a tube and then sew on the seat top and bottom, leaving a 10-inch gap in the top seam to stuff the pellets in.

14 Fill bag with pellets. Be careful not to overfill it or you will have trouble fitting it into your seat cover. Slipstitch the beanbag top closed. Push the bag into the seat cover and zip it shut.

Nature Quilt

DIFFICULTY
RATING: ★ ★

50 x 70 inches

This quilt is a European design of two coordinating pieces. The bottom is a wool blanket with bound edges that drape over the bed while the smaller top piece is a traditional French *édredon* quilted and printed with a simple leaf design.

The fabrics include a variety of recycled materials including bed sheets, old curtains, and blankets. The ideal time to make this quilt is in the fall when you can collect fallen leaves to press and use as the stencil templates.

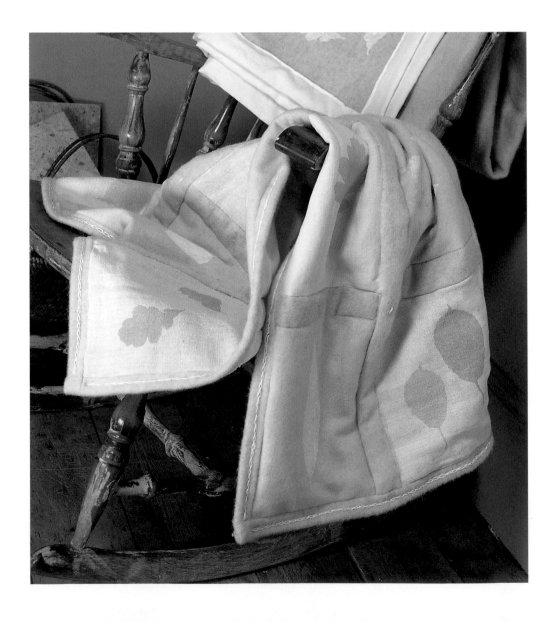

Materials

- *Scraps of plain white, cream, and gray fabrics in a variety of textures and weights for édredon blocks (not smaller than 9 x 10½ inches)*
- *Leaves*
- *Fabric paint*
- *½ yard of clear stencil plastic or stiff cardboard*
- *2 yards of 60-inch wide wool fabric*
- *2 yards of 60-inch wide white cotton fabric for édredon lining and blanket bindings*
- *1½ yards batting*
- *Assortment of embroidery threads*

Tools

- *Craft knife*
- *Stencil brush*
- *White paper plates*

Instructions

Note: All seam allowances are ⅝ inch unless otherwise stated.

STENCILING THE ÉDREDON BLOCKS

1 Cut twelve rectangles of 9 x 10½ inches from a variety of scrap fabrics.

2 Collect a selection of simple leaves and let them dry flat in a heavy book for a day. For each leaf, trace the outline on stencil plastic or stiff cardboard and cut out the stencil shape using a craft knife on a self-healing mat.

3 Prepare your work surface for stenciling by taping a sheet of plastic to the table. Lay one of the quilt blocks on top and tape a stencil to it.

4 Pour a tablespoon of fabric paint onto a paper plate and then pick up a little paint on the dry stencil brush. Blot the extra paint on a piece of paper. Pounce the brush through the stencil until you have covered the area with paint, picking up more paint as you need it. Let it dry and then remove the stencil and set the fabric paint according to the manufacturer's instructions. Repeat this process with different colored paints on the twelve quilt top blocks.

ASSEMBLING THE ÉDREDON

5 Cut nine strips of wool fabric 2½ x 10½ inches. Matching the 10½-inch sides, make three panels by alternating four stenciled quilt blocks with the strips. Press seams open.

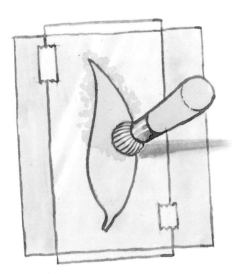

6 Cut four strips of wool fabric 2½ x 40 inches. Matching the 40-inch sides, sew the three panels together, alternating with the strips. Press the seams open.

7 Cut two strips of wool fabric 2½ x 32 inches. Sew these to the top and bottom of the *édredon*. Press seams open.

8 Bag out (see page 27 for technique) the *édredon* using a layer of the white cotton lining, two layers of batting, and the *édredon* top. Baste the layers together before quilting. After sewing the layers together as instructed, turn the quilt right side out and slipstitch the opening closed.

9 Stitch-in-the-ditch around each of the stenciled quilt blocks. Finish the border with a row of chain stitches using white embroidery thread. Remove all basting stitches.

MAKING THE UNDERBLANKET

10 Cut a 49 x 69-inch rectangle of wool fabric. Stencil one motif in each corner of the blanket.

11 From white cotton lining fabric, cut and piece enough strips of fabric to make a 4-inch wide binding, long enough to go around the blanket edge. Attach the binding (see page 28 for technique).

▼ *Collect leaves for making stencils on a fall walk with your child.*

Pressed Leaf Cloth Book

DIFFICULTY
RATING: ★

9 x 17 ½ inches

This is a project to make with kids. They can collect and identify leaves to use in the book and practice embroidery, appliqué, printing, and painting on fabric. The pages are made from two layers of fabric which are bound together down the center to form a book. A variety of printed and plain fabrics may be used.

Materials

- *Leaves*
- *Pencil*
- *Stencil plastic*
- *Scraps of fabrics*
- *Fabric paints*
- *Scraps of fusible bonding web*
- *Embroidery and sewing threads*
- *Decorative notions such as buttons, hooks, and ribbons*

Tools

- *Stencil brush*
- *Craft knife*
- *White paper plates*

COLLECTING AND PREPARING THE LEAVES

1 Collect a selection of simple leaves and let them dry flat in a heavy book for a day. You will be decorating the pages of your book by stenciling or appliquéing these leaf shapes onto each page. For each leaf, trace the outline onto stencil plastic and cut out the template stencil. Identify the different leaves so you can include the name of the leaf in the page decoration.

DECORATING THE PAGES

2 To make a book with six pages, cut six 9 x 17½-inch rectangles from different fabrics. Each page can be decorated using your leaf stencils and templates. Remember that the middle of the page will be the center of the book, where the binding stitches are, so do not decorate the middle inch-wide strip. You will only decorate the front of each page, which will then be quilted together with another page to create the opposite side.

3 To stencil, prepare your work surface by taping a plastic sheet to the table. Lay one of the fabric pages on top and tape a stencil to it. Pour a tablespoon of fabric paint onto a paper plate and then pick up a little paint on the dry stencil brush. Blot the extra paint on a piece of paper. Pounce the brush through the stencil until you have covered the area with paint, picking up more paint as you need it. Let it dry, then remove the stencil and set the fabric paint according to the manufacturer's instructions.

4 The leaf appliqués are double sided because they are loosely attached to the book and both sides may show. Trace your leaves on the fusible bonding web and apply it to the wrong side of a fabric. Carefully cut out the shape and remove the backing paper. Fuse the leaf shape to another fabric and then cut it out. Make a variety of leaf shapes and then tack them to pages of your book with simple embroidery stitches.

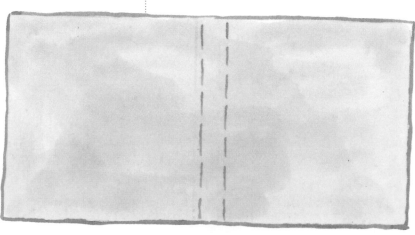

5 Write the names of the leaves in pencil on the pages and then embroider using a stem stitch. French knots and other embroidery stitches (see page 23 for techniques) can be used to embellish the pages, or you can stick or sew small notions on.

▲ *The leaves are placed randomly, reflecting a natural arrangement.*

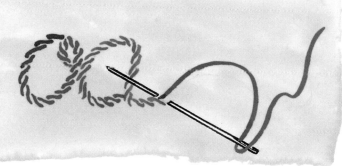

COMPLETING THE BOOK

6 When the pages are decorated, lay two wrong sides together, and zigzag around the outside edge to create a neat double-sided page. Lay all the pages flat on top of each other in the order you prefer and tie the book together at the center using three surgeon's square knots (see illustration right). Fold and press along the center to create the book binding.

Gingham Patch and Bow Quilt

DIFFICULTY
RATING: ✱ ✱

56 x 88 inches

This clever quilt makes a decorative feature of the ties that bind the quilt layers together by making them from rag bows cut with pinking shears. Gingham fabrics can easily be found in a variety of colors and check sizes. The alternating scale of the checks is what gives this quilt its dynamic look. To make a smaller quilt for a crib, decrease the number of blocks to achieve the size you want.

Materials

- 3½ yards of 45-inch ivory
  cotton for quilt backing
  and blocks
- ¼ yard each of red, lilac,
  yellow, green, and navy
  blue gingham
- Sewing thread
- ½ yard of fusible bonding
  web
- Scraps of colored cotton
  fabrics for the bows,
  pendants and heart
  appliqués
- 3 yards of 45-inch wide
  batting
- 9 yards of double-fold
  bias binding

Tools

- Pinking shears
- Pair of pliers
- Upholstery needle with a
  large eye

Instructions

*Note: All seam
allowances are ⅝ inch
unless otherwise stated.*

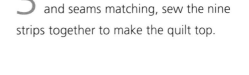

PIECING THE QUILT BLOCKS

1 Cut out 72 squares from ivory cotton
and 72 squares from the gingham
fabrics using template A on page 126.

2 Make nine strips consisting of 16
alternating ivory and gingham
patches by sewing one block to the next
with edges and right sides together. You
may prefer to lay out the entire quilt top
on the floor before you stitch the blocks
together to be sure you are happy with the
balance of colors and patterns. Press all
seams toward the gingham patches.

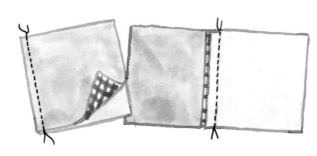

3 With edges and right sides together
and seams matching, sew the nine
strips together to make the quilt top.

▼ *The triangular pendants around the border will fall over the sides of the bed, giving it an interesting decorative element.*

COMPLETING THE QUILT TOP

4 Using the template on page 120, trace 41 triangle pendants on fusible bonding web. Iron the bonding to a variety of fabric scraps and cut out.

5 Iron the triangles onto different colored fabrics, leaving a border of at least ⅜ inch all around.

6 Zigzag around the two long edges of the triangle, leaving the short edge unstitched. Cut out the pendants close to the stitching.

7 Center a triangle pendant in the middle of each quilt block at the sides and bottom of the quilt top. With edges and right sides together, machine baste the triangles to the quilt top.

8 Make two 6½ x 88-inch strips from ivory fabric for the quilt side borders, joining sections where necessary. For the quilt bottom border, make one 6½ x 46½-inch piece from ivory fabric.

9 Trace the heart template on page 120 on the fusible bonding web and iron to the appliqué fabric. Fuse the heart shapes to the bottom of the side borders, leaving a gap of 1½ inches from the bottom and side edges. Zigzag around the heart edges.

10 With edges and right sides together and triangle pendants sandwiched between, sew the quilt bottom border to the quilt top. Press seam open. Repeat for the side borders.

TYING THE QUILT LAYERS

11 Baste the quilt layers together (see page 27 for technique).

12 Cut 72 strips of colored cotton fabrics 1 x 10 inches with pinking shears for the bows. As these may eventually fray, especially with washing, it would be advisable to keep some extra fabric to replace the bows when necessary.

13 To make a bow tie, thread a strip onto the upholstery needle. Push the needle down through the center of an ivory cotton block to the underside of the quilt. Use the pliers if necessary to pull the needle through. Insert the needle ⅜ inch away and pull it up to the right side of the quilt top, using the pliers to pull it through. Tie the rag into a knot and then a bow on the quilt top.

14 Bind the edges of the quilt (see page 28 for technique) with the double-fold bias binding and remove the basting stitches.

▼ *This quilt can be successfully coupled with the pillowcase project featured on page 112.*

Gingham Pillowcase

DIFFICULTY
RATING: ✱

19 x 27½ inches

This pillowcase matches the gingham patch and bow quilt and should fit most standard pillows. Make it from different fabrics to coordinate with other quilts in this book.

Materials

- ¼ yard of red gingham
- ½ yard of ivory cotton
- Scraps of gingham fabrics for triangle pendants
- Sewing thread

Instructions

Note: All seam allowances are ½ inch unless otherwise stated.

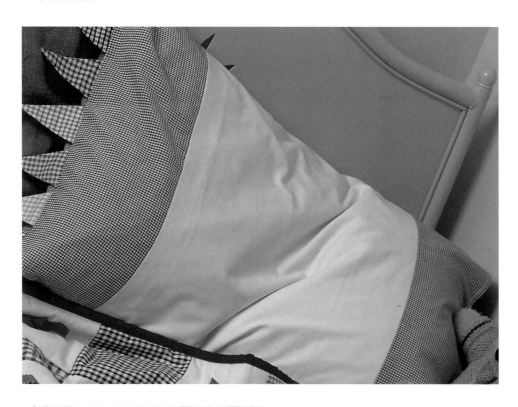

MAKING THE CASE FRONT AND BACK

1 Cut five 7 x 21-inch rectangles from gingham fabric and two 17 x 21-inch rectangles from ivory fabric.

2 With long edges and right sides together, make the front and back of the pillowcase by sewing a gingham rectangle to each side of an ivory one. Press all seams toward the gingham fabric.

3 Turn under a ½-inch hem along one gingham panel edge which will form the front opening.

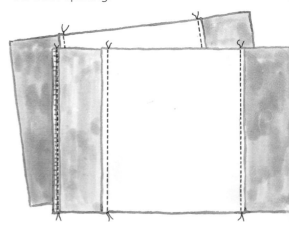

4 Turn under another ½-inch hem along the long side of the remaining gingham rectangle. With edges and right sides together, stitch the other side of the gingham rectangle to the back opening. Fold over to the wrong side.

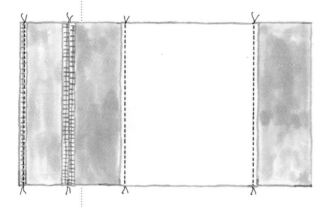

MAKING THE TRIANGLE PENDANTS

5 Make seven pendants from gingham fabric scraps by cutting two triangular shapes for each with the template on page 120. With edges and right sides together, sew each of the seven triangles together with a ¼-inch seam allowance, leaving the short side open. Clip the points off the seam allowance and turn the triangles right side out. Press seams flat.

6 Pin all the triangles an equal distance apart along the right side of the unhemmed gingham end of the pillowcase front. Machine baste in place.

7 With edges and right sides together, seams matching and triangle pendants sandwiched between the front and back, sew the sides and end of the pillowcase together. Clip the corners off the seam allowance and turn right side out.

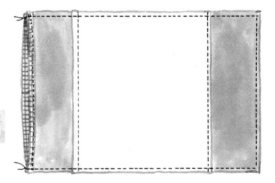

8 Cut four 1½ x 20-inch strips from gingham fabric for the ties. Press under a hem on all sides of each of the ties and edge-stitch in place. Sew one end of each tie to the front and back of the pillowcase, 6 inches from each side seam.

Gingham Bag

DIFFICULTY
RATING: ★ ★

16 inches high

A duffel bag for carrying kid's gear that looks equally good over a child or an adult shoulder is a rare and wonderful thing. Too often, fluffy pink bunny bags end up being toted around by parents. Bear this in mind when choosing the fabrics for this bag and you won't go wrong. The body and base of this bag are machine quilted to make it durable.

Materials

- ½ yard yellow gingham
- Scrap of fusible bonding web
- Threads to match appliqué, quilted gingham, and bag top
- 1 yard of cotton fabric for base and lining
- Scraps of colored cottons and gingham for appliqué and pendants
- ½ yard of batting
- ½ yard of muslin
- ¼ yard of cotton fabric for bag top

Instructions

Note: All seam allowances are ½ inch unless otherwise stated.

MAKING THE POCKET

1 Cut two 7½ x 8¼-inch rectangles of yellow gingham for the pocket and lining. Trace the star appliqué on page 120 on the fusible bonding web and iron it on the right side, in the center, of the pocket front. Zigzag stitch around the outside edge of the pocket.

2 With edges and right sides together, sew the lining to the pocket along all four sides, leaving 4 inches open along the bottom. Turn the pocket right side out and press. Turn under the remaining seam allowances and slipstitch together.

3 To make the pleats at the sides of pocket, make a fold 1 inch from each side and press them to meet the outside edge of the pocket. Baste in place.

QUILTING THE BAG

4 Cut a 14 x 32-inch rectangle from each of gingham, batting, and muslin. Layer them and baste together with the muslin on the bottom, batting in the middle, and the gingham right side up on the top.

5 Using the pattern piece for the base section on page 126, cut a base from each of the lining fabric, batting, and muslin. Layer and baste these as you did the gingham, placing the lining right side up on the top.

6 Machine-quilt the base in parallel lines 1½ inches apart.

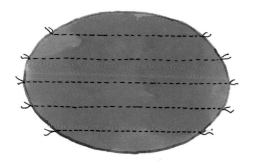

7 Machine-quilt the gingham in parallel lines 1 inch apart, using the gingham grid as a guide.

8 Edge-stitch the pocket to the center front of the bag, stitching in the pleat along the bottom edge of the pocket. Remove the basting from the pocket, gingham body, and bag base.

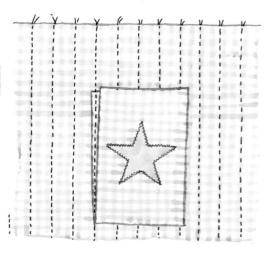

9 With edges and right sides together, sew the gingham body into a tube. With edges and right sides together, pin the base to the bottom of the body tube and sew in place. Trim and clip the seam allowances.

MAKING THE TRIANGLE PENDANTS

10 Make eight pendants from gingham scraps by cutting two triangular shapes for each using the template on page 120. With edges and right sides together, sew each triangle together making a ¼-inch seam allowance and leaving the short side open. Clip the points off the seam allowance and turn the triangles right side out. Press seams flat.

11 With edges together and triangle points facing down, pin all the pendants at equal intervals along the top of the gingham bag. Machine baste them in place.

▼ *Make the triangular ends of the drawstrings in a contrasting color, so that they show up against the side of the bag.*

MAKING THE BAG OPENING

12 For the bag top, cut a 7½ x 32-inch rectangle. Make it into a tube by sewing the short sides, matching edges and with right sides together.

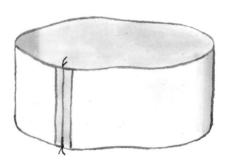

13 Sew the bag top to the gingham bag, edges and right sides together, matching the back seams and sandwiching the pendants. Press the seam allowance toward the bag top and topstitch, catching the seam allowance in the stitching. Iron the ½-inch hem allowance of the bag top to the wrong side of the fabric.

14 To make the drawstring casing, cut a strip of fabric 2¼ x 30 inches. Press the seam allowance under. Pin the strip along the center of the bag top. Edge-stitch along the length of the casing.

15 To make the drawstrings, cut a strip of fabric 1¾ x 45 inches. Fold in half lengthwise and turn under the seam allowances, then edge-stitch. Thread through the casing with a safety pin, then complete each end of the drawstring by attaching a stuffed triangle. Make the triangle as you did in step 10, adding a layer of batting between. Turn under the ¼-inch seam allowance along the short end of the triangle. Insert the drawstring into the triangle and stitch in place, repeat for the other end.

ASSEMBLING THE LINING

16 For the bag lining, cut out a 21 x 32-inch rectangle and cut another bag base from the pattern piece on page 126. Assemble the bag lining as you did the bag. Iron the ½-inch hem allowance at the top to wrong side.

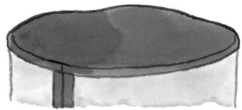

17 Insert the lining into bag with wrong sides together. Slipstitch the top of the bag to the lining.

▼ *When you pull the drawstrings, the pendants stand up from the side of the bag, adding a lively decorative touch.*

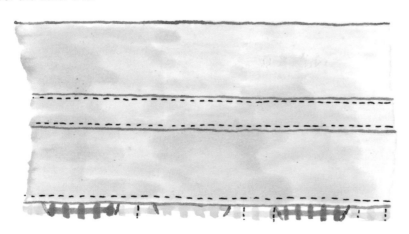

Dalmatian Fur Quilt

DIFFICULTY
RATING: ★

50 x 50 inches

Fake furs come in many different qualities and prints, including tiger, giraffe, and Dalmatian imitations. Choose one that is machine washable and not too heavy. This quilt is backed with polar fleece, which makes it easy to sew and very cozy. The dimensions of this quilt can easily be changed to accommodate any size bed.

Materials

- *1¾ yards of fake fur fabric, at least 44 inches wide*
- *1¾ yards of orange polar fleece, at least 45 inches wide*
- *1¾ yards of ocher polar fleece, at least 45 inches wide*
- *Ocher thread*

Instructions

Note: All seam allowances are ¾ inch unless otherwise stated.

1 Cut rectangles of 42½ x 62½ inches from the fake fur and the orange polar fleece. Pin the fabrics with edges and wrong sides together; then baste ½ inch from the edge.

2 Cut two 11 x 63-inch strips from the ocher polar fleece for bindings. Place these strips, edges and right sides together, along the long side edges of the fake fur. Machine stitch in place.

3 Fold the bindings in half so they enclose the quilt seam allowances. Then, turning under the seam allowance, pin, covering the machine stitches. Hem the binding in place.

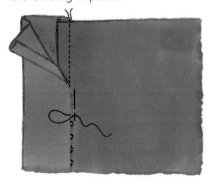

4 Cut two 11 x 52-inch strips from ocher polar fleece for the top bindings. Place these strips edges and right sides together on top of the fake fur and fleece binding at the top and bottom edges of the quilt. Machine stitch in place.

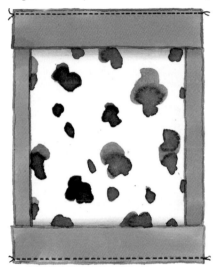

5 Fold the bindings in half so they enclose the quilt and side bindings and then turn under the seam allowance and pin, covering the machine stitches. Slipstitch in place, enclosing the ends of the top and bottom binding.

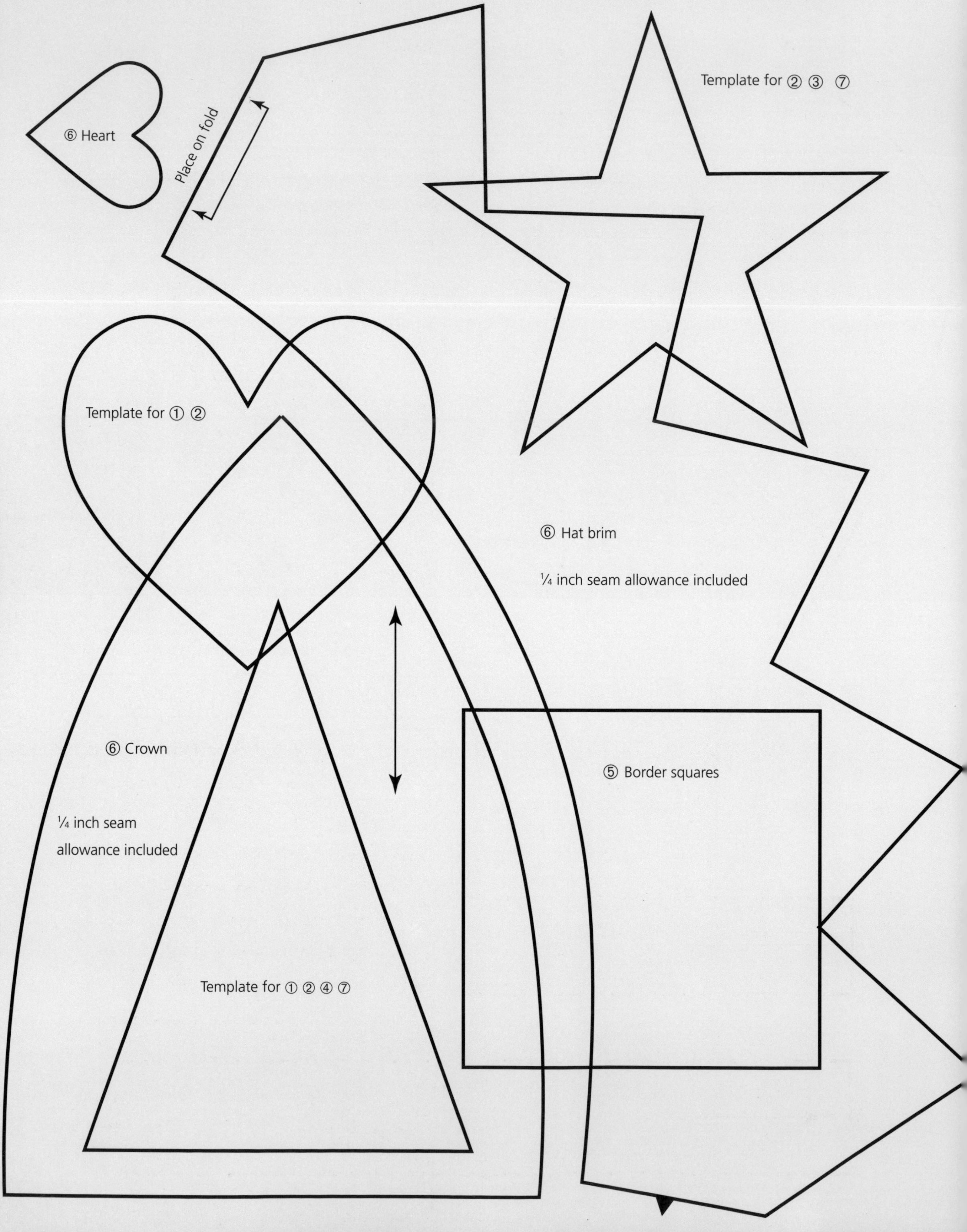

⑥ Heart

Place on fold

Template for ② ③ ⑦

Template for ① ②

⑥ Hat brim

¼ inch seam allowance included

⑥ Crown

¼ inch seam
allowance included

⑤ Border squares

Template for ① ② ④ ⑦

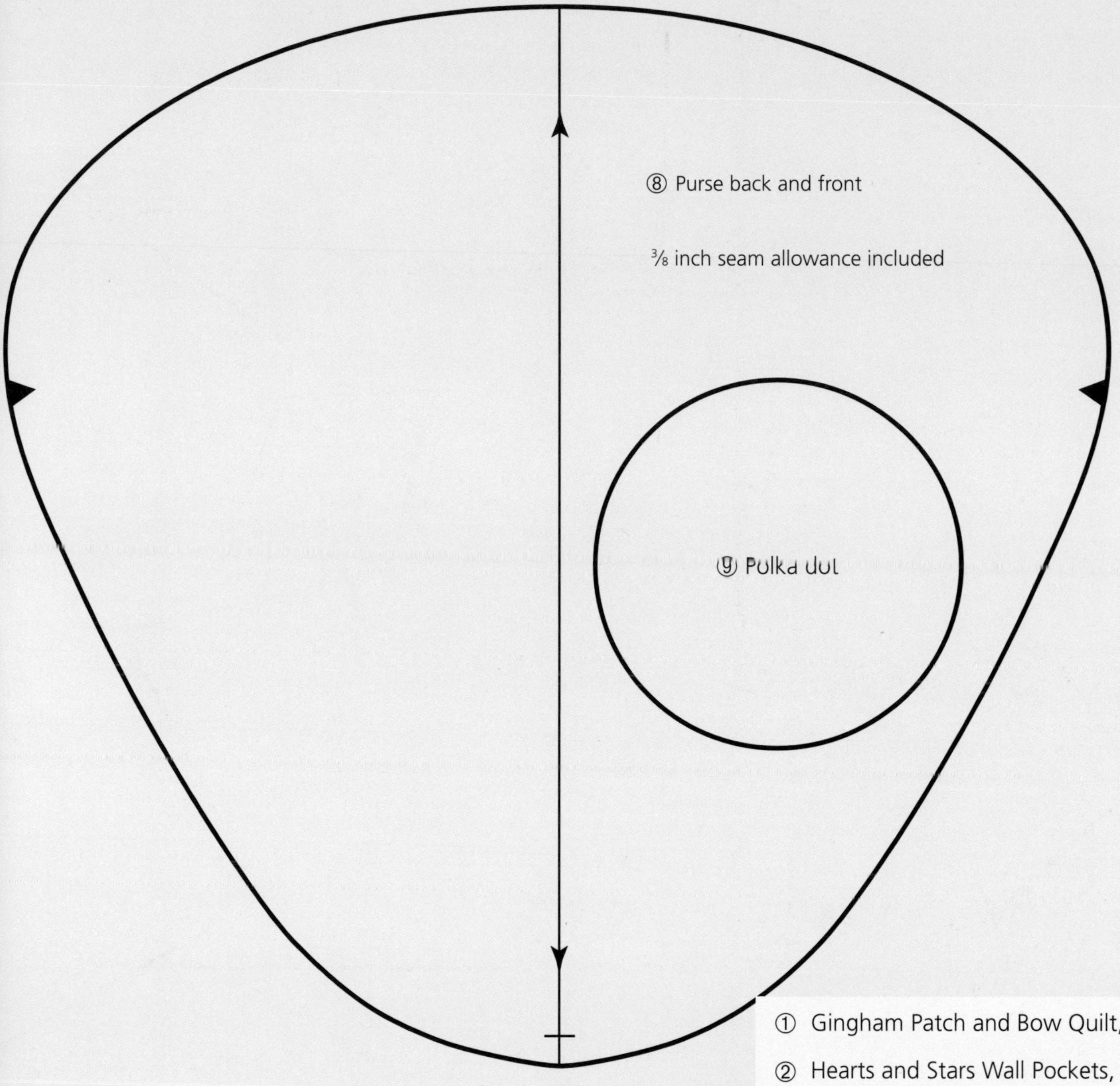

⑧ Purse back and front

⅜ inch seam allowance included

⑨ Polka dot

① Gingham Patch and Bow Quilt, see pages 108-111

② Hearts and Stars Wall Pockets, see pages 35-37

③ Beanbag Seat, see pages 98-101

④ Gingham Pillowcase, see pages 112-113

⑤ Tree of Life Quilt, see pages 32-34

⑥ Hearts Hat, see pages 81-83

⑦ Gingham Bag, see pages 114-117

⑧ Little Bird Purse, see pages 51-53

⑨ Humpty-Dumpty Quilt, see pages 62-65

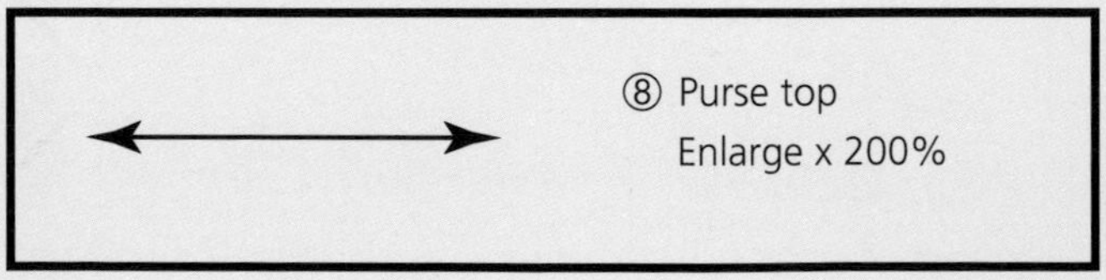

⑧ Purse top
Enlarge x 200%

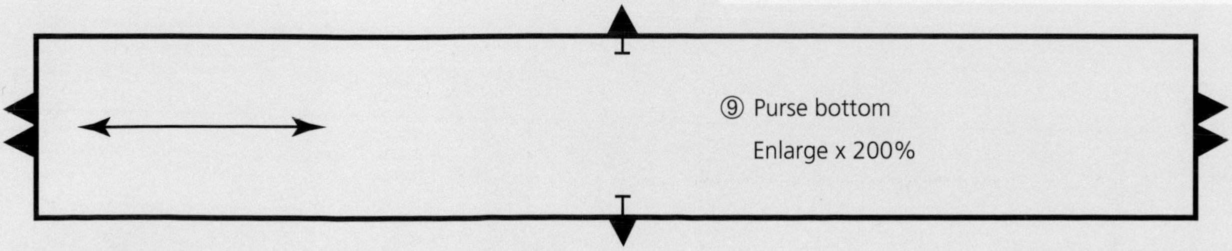

⑨ Purse bottom
Enlarge x 200%

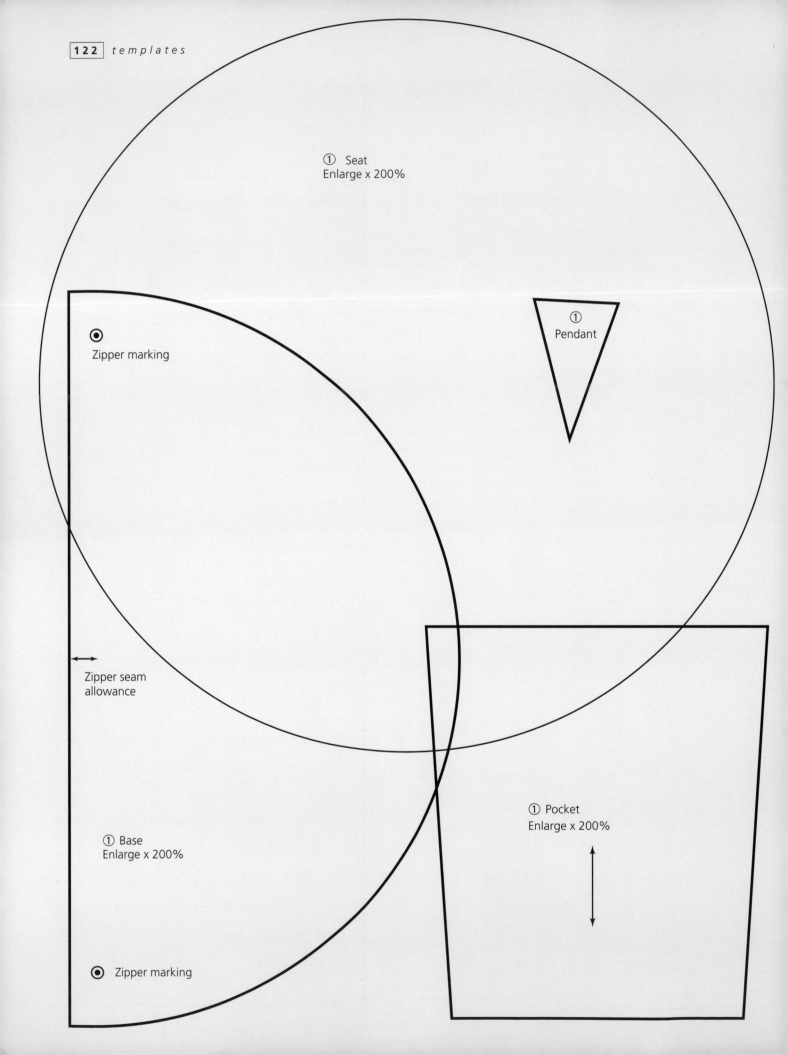

① Seat
Enlarge x 200%

① Pendant

⊙
Zipper marking

Zipper seam
allowance

① Pocket
Enlarge x 200%

① Base
Enlarge x 200%

⊙ Zipper marking

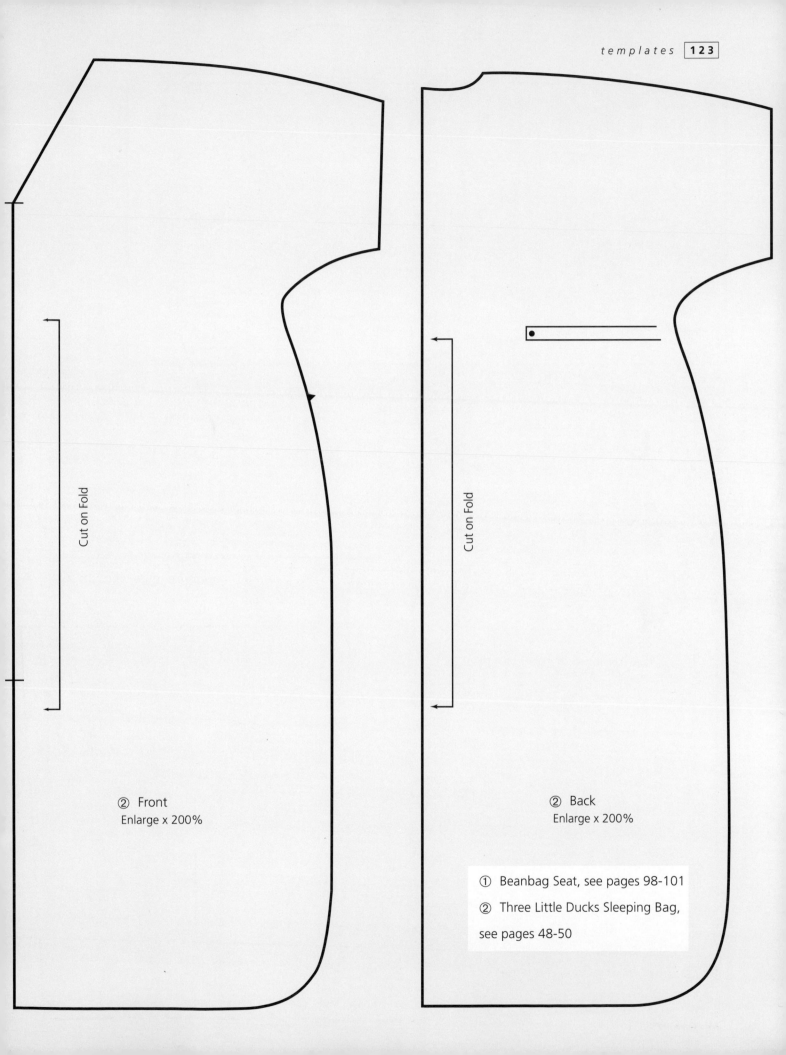

Cut on Fold

② Front
Enlarge x 200%

Cut on Fold

② Back
Enlarge x 200%

① Beanbag Seat, see pages 98-101

② Three Little Ducks Sleeping Bag,
see pages 48-50

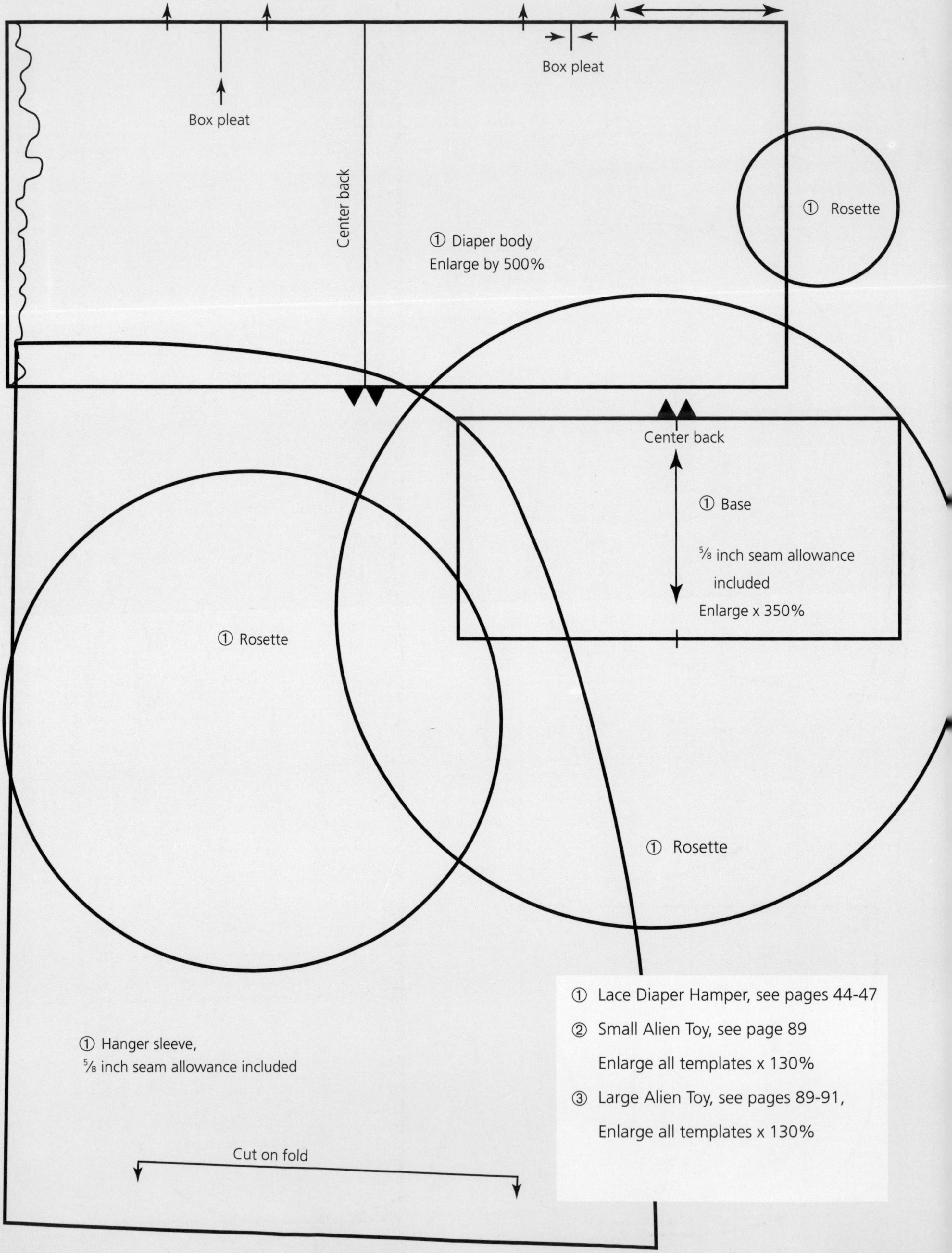

Box pleat

Box pleat

Center back

① Diaper body
Enlarge by 500%

① Rosette

Center back

① Base

⅝ inch seam allowance
included
Enlarge x 350%

① Rosette

① Rosette

① Hanger sleeve,
⅝ inch seam allowance included

Cut on fold

① Lace Diaper Hamper, see pages 44–47

② Small Alien Toy, see page 89
   Enlarge all templates x 130%

③ Large Alien Toy, see pages 89–91,
   Enlarge all templates x 130%

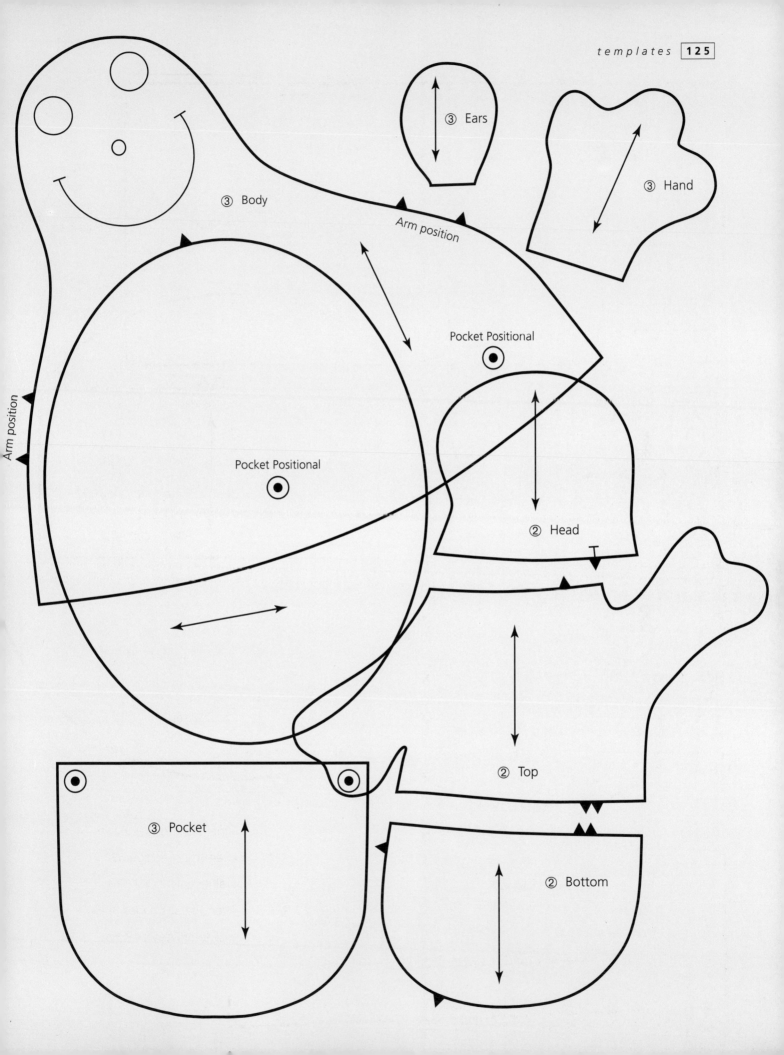

③ Ears

③ Hand

③ Body

Arm position

Pocket Positional

Arm position

Pocket Positional

② Head

② Top

③ Pocket

② Bottom

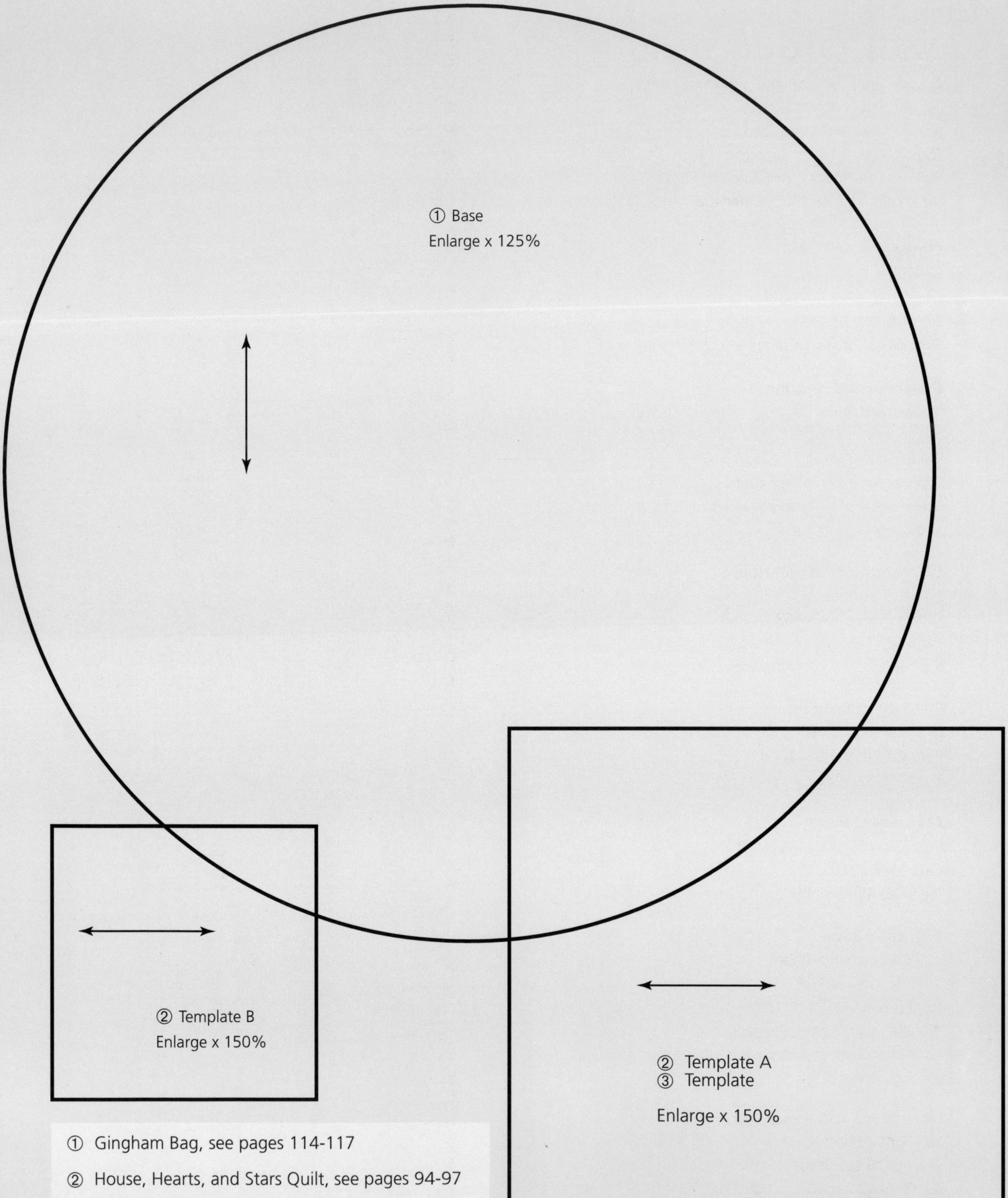

① Base
Enlarge x 125%

② Template B
Enlarge x 150%

② Template A
③ Template

Enlarge x 150%

① Gingham Bag, see pages 114-117

② House, Hearts, and Stars Quilt, see pages 94-97

③ Gingham Patch and Bow Quilt, see pages 108-111

Mail Order Suppliers

A wide variety of solid and patterned fabrics, quilting supplies, and notions are available through craft and fabric stores, and specialized mail-order suppliers. The website, http://quilt.com, is a good source of quilting information, including a listing of quilting supply stores throughout Canada and the U.S.

Clotilde
B3000
Louisiana, MO 63353-3000
Tel: (1-800) 772 2891
Suppliers of sewing notions, equipment and books.

Dover Publications, Inc.
31 East 2nd Street
Mineola, NY 11501
Tel: (516) 294 7000   Fax: (516) 742 6953
Supplier of books of alphabets, monograms, and other useful copyright-free images as well as books on quilting and other craft subjects.

EZ International/Quilt House
95 Mayhill Street
Saddle Brook, NJ 07663
Tel: (201) 712 1234   Fax: (201) 712 1199
Supplier of books and quilting notions.

The Fabric Stash
643 East 59th Street
Kansas City, MO 64110
Tel: (816) 523 7882   Fax: (816) 523 5922

Jan made Quilting
Box 514, 710 Montana Street
Circle, MT 59215
Tel: (406) 485 3694

Jillybean's Pride
222 Lakeshore Road East
Oakville, ON L6J 1H6
Tel and Fax: (905) 844 1793
Website: http://www.jillybeans.com
Hand-dyed fabrics, photo transfer paper, notions and quilting accessories.

Marge's Fabric & Fancy's Inc.
205 Yonge Street North
Stroud, ON L0L 2M0
Tel: (705) 431 3698   Fax: (705) 431 7905
Website: http://www3.sympatico.ca/marges.fabric.fancys
Specialises in 100% cotton fabrics, notions, patterns, books and quilting accessories. Catalog available.

Quilter's Garden
931 Kingston Road
Toronto, ON M4E 1S6
Tel: (416) 693 1616
Website: http://www.quiltersgarden.com
Fabric collections and quilting accessories.

Quilters' Line
57 Main Street West
Markdale, ON N0C 1H0
Tel: (519) 986 2244   Fax: (519) 986 4329
Website: http://www.quiltersline.com
Patterns, quilting notions and fabric collections, including lWilliam Morris, Shelburne Museum and 1930s reproductions.

Quilts and Other Comforts
1 Quilters Lane, Box 4100
Golden, CO 80402-4100
Tel: (1-800) 881 6624
Supplier of quilts.

The Secret Workshop
Box 31
Silverton, BC V0G 2B0
Tel: (205) 358 7902
Website: http://www.netidea.com/~workshop
Specialises in colorful fabrics for children, including cotton, interlock, flannelette, jersey, fleece, and denim. Swatched catalog available.

ACKNOWLEDGMENTS

The Author would like to thank Nancy Nicholson and Carol Collet for their project design contributions. Nancy designed and made the Tree of Life Quilt; Birds and Hearts Mobile; Hearts and Stars Wall Pockets; Animal Quilt; Hearts Hat; House, Hearts, and Stars Quilt; Beanbag Seat; Gingham Patch and Bow Quilt; Gingham Bag; and Gingham Pillowcase. Carol contributed the designs and examples of the Nature Quilt and the Pressed Leaf Cloth Book. The Publishers would like to thank Strawberry Fayre for offering a discount on their materials and to Cheong Interiors for kindly lending some blankets featured in the photographs.

Index